Hearing Young People Talk About Witnessing Domestic Violence

Exploring Feelings, Coping Strategies and Pathways to Recovery

Susan Collis

Foreword by Gill Hague

Jessica Kingsley

First published in 2013
by Jessica Kingsley Publishers
116 Pentonville Road
London N1 9JB, UK
and
400 Market Street, Suite 400
Philadelphia, PA 19106, USA

www.jkp.com

Library of Congress Cataloging in Publication Data
Collis, Susan, 1948-
  Listening to young people who have experienced domestic violence / Susan Collis.
    p. cm.
  Includes bibliographical references and index.
  ISBN 978-1-84905-378-5 (alk. paper)
  1. Family violence. 2. Victims of family violence--Rehabilitation. 3. Youth and violence. 4. Abused children. I. Title.
  HV6626.C647 2012
  362.82'92--dc23
                            2012031796

British Library Cataloguing in Publication Data
A CIP catalogue record for this book is available from the British Library

ISBN 978 1 84905 378 5
eISBN 978 0 85700 735 3

Printed and bound in Great Britain

Contents

Foreword

I am pleased to write the foreword for this interesting and creative addition to the literature on young people and domestic violence. Building on an innovative, reflexive study, the book uses in-depth interviews with young people which are then sympathetically drawn out to build a graceful and powerful analysis of their stories.

A brave, unusual book in many ways, it presents hidden and silenced voices, full of hurt and trauma – but in the end, in some cases anyway, leading to peace, hopefulness and resolution. The often courageous and painful journeys described lie at the heart of insightful contributions from the author, adding to our understanding of the devastating impacts domestic abuse can have on children and young people.

Sue Collis categorises the voices of the young people as 'knowing', 'hurting' or 'suffering', and 'healing'. Sometimes the voices are agonised, confused and guilty, sometimes aggressive but always complex, leading into the multiple strands which make up each story of a person, still more or less at the beginning of their life, but traumatised and struggling to transcend abusive experiences.

This issue of domestic violence began to come to the fore in the 1970s and 1980s. However, it was not until the 1990s that the effects on children experiencing, or living with, domestic violence between their parents or carers began to gain attention in this country, with key texts by Audrey Mullender, Liz Kelly, Caroline McGee, Ravi Thiara and Cathy Humphreys, among others, as well as Marianne Hester, Ellen Malos, myself and associates in the Centre for Gender and Violence Research at the University of Bristol. These texts began to right previous wrongs in terms of the scandalous ignoring of domestic violence in child protection cases as well as the issue of neglect in general in the past. Children and young people carried their pain from their domestic violence experiences without anyone much showing the slightest interest.

Now things have changed. Domestic violence is an issue of child protection concern and there are at least some services, both in refuges and elsewhere (although limited and often with threatened funding). There have been various research studies and books. Some of these have begun the project of raising, and learning from, the actual expressed voices of children and young people.

This new book is in this tradition. However, it takes the subject further in terms of the detailed and perceptive analysis presented, and the respect and 'highlighting' accorded to each young person's story and their own view of their story. The book leads on to suggest ways in which such profound and careful listening to young people can lead to improving and deepening practical responses by domestic violence services, activists, social workers, practitioners and policy makers. The resulting suggestions aim to meet the needs of such damaged young people and work towards transformative approaches. Looking at each person's story in multiple ways, leads us, then, to begin to understand the depth and complexity involved which, as helping adults and practitioners, we need to learn to address. The book provides gentle and moving insights and ways forward, responding sensitively to the individual struggles of the young people which were sometimes heroic.

In fact, my own view is that children who experience or live with domestic abuse are often 'heroes of their own lives', but commonly no-one else recognises this – even now. This moving contribution is part of shifting the ground towards those young people, and providing information and insights for professionals and domestic violence survivors themselves. We need to be very grateful to Sue Collis for this unique book. But most of all, our thanks to the young people who courageously shared their stories and pain. The author calls them 'valiant, and indeed they are. Let us try to learn from them.

Emeritus Professor Gill Hague
Professor of Violence Against Women Studies
Centre for Gender and Violence Research
University of Bristol

Introduction

'It's OK to Talk'

It seems like a statement of the obvious if we hear someone saying, 'It's ok to talk.' However, it is probable that, in the context of lives steeped in domestic violence, the full significance of what is being said is lost to us. In the framework of experiences of domestic violence, we need to be reminded that, in the past, there has often been a pervasive, all-consuming silence which has permeated everything to do with domestic violence. It would appear that it's *not* been ok to talk. However, there is no desire here to undervalue in any way the tireless efforts which have taken place in this country and others to research the consequences of domestic violence, and break the silence. The courageous efforts of survivors together with researchers are acknowledged and seen as crucial and far-reaching.

Despite these developments, domestic violence occurring in individuals' lives may still remain private and hidden, and may stay locked in the home, where it has been perpetrated, perpetuated and silenced. The reasons for this are complex and dependent on varied influences and factors.

I offer here a woman's view which is particular in that it is my view, but it does also contain ideas which have been offered to me by other women, who are, like me, survivors.

Historically, women have remained silent because they may think they are to blame for the abuse; they may think they deserve such treatment; they may think that they have to accept it as part of life; they may be too ashamed to talk; they may hope that things will get better, that somehow the man they love will change; they may believe that no one cares or is interested; they may have been coerced into believing that they have made their bed and they must lie on it; they may be just too terrified to talk because they have been intimidated over a protracted period and threatened with appalling consequences; they may fear for their children and think that if they expose the violence they will be held responsible, and their children will be taken away; they may not realise that they are being abused and do not see what is happening as in any way wrong; they may accept the abuse because they are so controlled and have become so powerless that they do not have the confidence or self-belief to make a simple decision like talking to someone; they may believe they are loved by the perpetrator and remain loyal to him; they may love the perpetrator and do not want to expose his abuse because some of the time he is a caring partner and that's what really counts; they may think there is no one they can talk to; they may believe that talking will make things worse; they may be strongly influenced by their particular family culture which states that disgrace is always associated with disclosures of domestic violence. There are many varied, complex reasons why women remain silent.

I began my years of abuse with fourteen years of silence for some of these reasons. I have realised that the silence was intrinsically damaging and that I allowed the abuse to go on for much longer than it should have done, and the silence was responsible, in large measure, for my entrapment. It provided the backdrop for further abusive relationships which followed in succession, mainly due to the harm caused by the first relationship when I had remained silent. My silence confined me to a dungeon which kept me apart from any support I might have received. In 1984, after 14 years, I disclosed the abuse to my doctor, another woman. I remember how shocked she was when I shared a small fragment of the abuse. It went no further. I was not offered any support. I was expected to carry on living as if nothing had happened. I couldn't.

The consequence was another eighteen years of domestic violence with other partners, utterly eroding any vestiges of self-worth I might have had.

I do not intend to dwell on my experiences, except to make the critical observation that talking about experiences of domestic violence brings untold rewards, as well as possessing the potential of eradicating what I see as the dire consequences of remaining silent.

I do want to stress the importance of specialised support services for victims and survivors of domestic violence. I, like all victims, needed to be helped by someone who had the ability to understand and was able to empathise with the unique kind of suffering associated with domestic violence. To be suffering at the hands of someone who is supposed to be loving and caring, in a place, the home, which should be the safest and most secure place in our lives, has peculiar and distinctive consequences which some might have difficulty understanding. For example, the question, 'Why don't you leave?' is asked by someone who has no insight into the plight of those women who hopelessly hope that the suffering will end, but remain trapped in abusive relationships. Women do not leave for a vast number of credible reasons, many of which are tied up with the reasons for remaining silent.

Perhaps we would do well to reflect on the situation of an abused woman, feeling powerless, unconfident and afraid, probably with dependent children, possibly friendless and isolated, with little or no financial independence or personal means, with no particular place to go, and then think that it is a remarkable thing that some women actually do leave.

Silence does perpetuate suffering and abuse. I did find my voice. Once I had found it, I wanted to make it possible for others, particularly children and young people, to be heard.

This book is a voice for five young people who wanted their stories to be heard. They speak of their experiences in individual ways, and each has bravely reflected on their lives and support the idea that, as Rose said: '…it's ok to talk.' I had the great privilege of meeting with these young people, and they shared with me their stories. I then spent time reflecting on what they had said, trying to give their stories the attention and the thought they deserved. I noticed a lot of things which I felt were significant and I learnt a lot. Finally, I thought about these young people in relation to all the children and young people we know who are in need of support and help, and I wondered if I could apply something of what I had learnt to them. I concluded that I could, and that other people could also.

I have chosen to dwell on my thoughts in relation to the stories I had heard. I had embarked on a piece of research which soon became more than that. The stories are powerful and provoke many ideas and concepts. Every kind of verbal statement is included because of its value in its own right and also because each had the potential to act as a springboard to think about a much broader context. What we learn about one individual's life may lead us to learn about another's, and work towards a fuller understanding of every child and young person who we have the privilege and honour to meet. I hope the stories of these five young people will inspire the reader to try a little harder at understanding other children's and young people's stories.

Each chapter contains an overall view and discussion of the overarching theme of the chapter. This is to set the findings of the research into a wider context and to enlighten the reader in relation to a broader evidence base. The findings of other research and the ideas and theories of those who have contributed to the development of knowledge associated with each of the main themes will be discussed.

Chapter 1 introduces the young people, whose names have been changed. They are Scott, Coral, Terry, Karl and Rose, and who give their stories of domestic violence. From their stories, 'sketches' have been drawn for each young person, to give some insight into their experiences, and these provide the foundation on which later interpretations and descriptions are based. This chapter also describes the invaluable contribution a young person's story makes in understanding and supporting her or him. Being able to listen and compile a story is a precious occupation, which may bring untold rewards in the way of understanding and supporting the giver of the story. How the stories were gathered is related, providing general guidance to those who would wish to work with children and young people in this way.

Chapter 2 is shaped by each individual voice and is centred on how each young person expresses their unique voice and identity in relation to their experiences and impressions of domestic violence. Their voices are identified in terms of their feelings, their understanding and their individual experiences. A discussion is included about the significance of 'voice', and what may be available to those of us who want to reflect on the essence of a person's story. Making inferences and interpretations begin to gain momentum, and the stories take on deeper meanings and considerations. Conclusions are drawn as to the overall 'voice' of each young person, and there follow reflections on the possible value of this and what it might do to assist the listener in informing his or her practice. Being able to recognise the essence of a person's voice is discussed in relation to professional practice and personal relationships.

Chapter 3 is devoted to the young people's emotionality and the journey each has taken through disempowering emotions through to humanising empowering emotions, as they have endured suffering and have found their means of expression from hurting to healing. Recognising an emotional journey is seen as prerequisite to understanding the person.

The drama and power contained in feelings is acknowledged, and the value of becoming aware of where a young person is on the journey is emphasised. How to gather emotional knowledge is discussed, alongside the evidence to support the need for professional practice to encompass this aspect of experience. Evidence is cited which emphasises the need for professionals to take on a significant amount of responsibility in ensuring the emotional and psychological wellbeing of young people, by being equipped to offer some form of diagnosis and appropriate support to those who are in their care.

Chapter 4 describes and interprets the young people's ways of coping with their experiences of domestic violence. This chapter also introduces the concept of 'waves of resilience', and argues that if professionals and others can become aware of what each child and young person uses to wash away the adverse effects of domestic violence, or any protracted trauma for that matter, it would assist them in being able to pin down what might be encouraged to strengthen those they support. Pathways to coping competency are discussed in this context.

Chapter 5 is allocated to the young people's individual views towards those with whom they have associated, drawing attention to those relationships which have impacted upon them, and which proved significant to them. The building of relationships is crucial to all, within families and between professionals and individuals and groups. All that we do, I would venture to say, is dependent upon it, and as a result, the chapter looks at the broader significance of the hallmarks of a sustaining and empowering relationship with a child or young person. Recent evidence is explained in support of those wider relationships which could have a significant bearing on the accomplishments of young people.

Chapter 6 focuses on the spiritual yearnings of the young people and how they express their desires, and aspire for something higher and better in their lives. For some the discussion here might be a surprise. However, evidence of spirituality remains in the stories, and as such was recognised, discussed and viewed in the light of the broader context of acknowledging aspirations of faith.

Chapter 7, the concluding chapter, entitled 'Helping into Wholeness', seeks to provide the beginnings of a discussion around the most relevant and empowering ways that can be used to assist young people on their journeys through suffering and beyond. The chapter concludes with a series of suggestions which are listed as 'provisions', which may assist anyone considering improvements in their support of children and young people. They are provisions which I hope will be for consideration, and are, in some measure, supported by findings from broader research.

The book aims to describe the young people's individual voices, the emotionality of their journeys, their significant attempts at forming important relationships, their attempts at coping and their spiritual yearnings, but within each chapter an effort has been made to configure these specific interpretations with the findings of others, so as to broaden understandings beyond the confines of a few individuals; the emphasis is placed on echoes, dissonances, parallels and contrary views in order for the reader to gain a fuller vision of young people's experiences. This will hopefully provoke further thoughts and ideas amongst those of us who want to improve our practice, so that we can support and assist children and young people in ways which reflect their wishes, feelings and thoughts. Support needs to be provided which captures their expressed desires, and which meets their needs.

Theories which inform those who are working with children and young people who have experienced domestic abuse will be discussed in the light of the stories here revealed. Additionally, it is the purpose of this book to clarify and encourage those aspects of support and experience which have proved, to these young people and to others, to be of the greatest benefit. These are those which have apparently undermined and sometimes eradicated the negative influences and effects of the past, and as such need to be remembered, applied and celebrated.

CHAPTER 1

Stories

Stories are the closest we can come to experience as we and others tell of our experience. A story is a broad, constructed narrative which is linguistic in form and presupposes a narrator and a listener whose different viewpoints affect the way the story is told and interpreted (Greenhalgh 1999).

The value of the story lies in the possibility of the construction of something entirely unique, the 'telling of our own tale', which questions the idea of a single, objective reality (Roberts 2002), and broadens and elaborates the meanings and understandings of life experience. Stories establish individuality and are open-ended, inconclusive and ambiguous (Denzin 1989). However, the collection and interpretation of storied lives leads in some measure to a grasp of difference and congruity, of similarities and conflict, of discrepancies and commonalities (Kiesinger 1998). The ambiguities, vagaries and complexities of lived experience are viewed in some measure in an articulated story, and the multi-dimensional aspects of our existence surface and become apparent, providing a view of a life lived, and an opportunity to interpret and analyse the most intimate and deep aspects of a life.

The intimate knowledge provided by the recounting and recording of stories is valuable, enlightening, powerful and authentic (Bolton 2005). Authenticity is linked to the expressions of individuals who have lived their lives and have shared their myriad thoughts, ideas, perceptions, emotions, hopes, images and observations, gleaned from their own unique and peculiarly personal experiences. Their testimonies possess a first-hand reality, an integrity and trustworthiness which is undeniable (Jessop and Penny 1999).

An overview of each young person's story is presented as an outline which was spoken in answer to questions which asked about their families, their homes and their experiences. For these outlines to be effective as clear and simple accounts, the voices of the young people cannot be directly heard at this time. This chapter is setting the scene and as such is devoid of 'talk'. The opening of a great drama must provide the context in which it is set. The places, the times, the characters on stage are introduced, and only then can the drama unfold through the script. The stories were constructed in the same way as a précis exercise in that the original interviews were recorded and then listened to many times. After a period of reflection, the question was asked, 'What are the main points being made?' Then while the words of the young person are ringing in the mind, the main points are listed and joined together in a logical way. That is to say, they are linked according to their relationship one with another.

Those conversations we have where there is no recording device need to be handled in the same way. Just as professionals are called upon to record interactions, and reflect upon their meaning and be analytical in their approach, this methodology can be applied to any initial interpretation of a story revealed. It is true that we cannot listen again and again. All the more reason to listen very acutely the first time – much may depend upon it.

It may be possible to take notes with the young person's consent. This would assist in deciphering the main points, enabling the later construction of the bare bones. As you read the following stories, it might be helpful to view them in the light of being like the laying of the first stone in the foundation of a great building. As such they are essential, but they form only a very small part of the whole.

The young people's names have been altered so as to protect their identities. Places and names are omitted to avoid any possibility of identification.

Scott

Scott was 13 years old at the time he shared his story. The domestic violence went on for a long time, several years in Scott's life. He had protected his younger brothers and sisters by taking them out of the danger. Sometimes, he was prompted to intervene, but feelings of fear would sometimes prevent him. He had seen his mother hurt. He had felt that he knew when the violent episodes were going to happen, and this had been 'weird'. He had thought when he was younger that domestic violence was acceptable, and he had been abusive to his mother. His awakening to the error of his thinking came suddenly when the police were called to his home because of his violent behaviour. He was put in a police cell for a time and had decided to change his behaviour; this had been successfully achieved as he had been told by more than one support worker that he had really improved.

He had learnt to value his experiences, and wanted to use them to help others. He had gained knowledge of how to support other people from one teacher in particular, and he had found that he was good at emulating what he had received, and making a difference to people around him. He had been instrumental in helping young people with problems using the methods employed by those who had supported him. He viewed these skills as something he would take into the future by becoming a support worker. At present he is happy at home; the perpetrator has been gone for some time. School is improving as he supports his friends, although he admits he finds the work at school to be problematic and difficult still. He has found strategies which have helped him deal with his feelings. He has used drawing and time-out to express and dispel powerful emotions. He feels more in control, and is enjoying family life. One aspect has been to go to church with his family and he believes in personal prayer.

Coral

Coral was 14 years old when she shared her story. Coral played a crucial part in her family's life. It was clear that her opinion was in the end a significant factor which made a huge difference to the way her mother saw their situation. Coral describes how her family had stayed together because her mother felt that staying together was the best option for the children. Despite things getting so bad that her mother had left the father, taking the children, more than once, and had gone into a refuge at least once but then had returned, Coral considered her role in the final decision to leave and not go back as being central to her mother's decision. There is a strong feeling that Coral's opinion was so important to her mother, that her voicing of her belief that her mother should leave for good was a turning point in the family. This resulted in action which was never gone back on. It is a very strong element which is reflected throughout her story. Her relationship with her mother possessed a closeness which appears to go beyond the boundaries of a mother/daughter relationship.

Coral's independence of people outside her mother and brothers is also a strong element, and there seems to be a lack of need, or a profession to the effect, for anyone else to be involved in her life while the family was going through very difficult experiences. Coral had tried to support her younger brothers and her mother, but had recognised that her involvement in the domestic violence had made things worse for her mother. Again this was a deciding factor in what she had decided to do. The details of her life are not dwelled upon, except in one or two exceptional instances.

Generally, Coral responds to her experiences in ways which demonstrate her maturity in emotional and psychological terms. She reflects upon her witnessing the domestic violence in calm and matter-of-fact ways without dwelling on any particular experiences; this appears to highlight her acceptance and acknowledgement of negative experiences in the light of her concern for her mother. Her own wishes appear to come about through the strength she has accumulated as she responded in vigilant and caring ways to her younger brothers and to her mother. She is able to state and act upon what she thinks is right, and accepts the consequences of her actions without complaint or regret. She is satisfied with her life with her family as it has become, and although there is no reference to her step-father, it is clear from her expressions of acceptance that she is apparently content with what has come about.

Terry

Terry was 13 years old at the time of his retelling his story. Terry has a troubled story which centres on his witnessing of his mother's suffering caused by appalling domestic violence. His story is not sequential, in that there seems to be a lack of continuity as far as events are concerned, but the images he creates, for example of him trying to push his father off his mother, his description of the domestic violence perpetrated against his sister's boyfriend and his father's behaviour in various settings are all vividly explained and described, creating powerful impressions.

Terry has remained close to his mother throughout the changes that have taken place. His loyalty is to her and to his family who are sympathetic to her and to her experiences. He is absolutely clear in his mind about what it was that brought about the violence against his mother and himself, and has no doubt that in some measure the controlling purpose of the violence has continued beyond his parents' separation. His emotional state is underpinned by a strong sense of injustice, which he sees as permeating and dominating the experiences of his family since the break-up. Despite the improvement in his mother's health which he has observed, in that the awful physical and mental abuse has ceased and she is no longer crying continuously, and is no longer suffering physical harm, he is aware that there are forces beyond her control which oppose her, and which anger and bewilder him. A very important aspect for him is that a degree of sympathy is shown to his father, which he sees as undeserving. He cannot conceal his contempt for those who make judgements which he sees as unfair and unsupported by the reality of their lives.

The relationships which he prizes are based upon the recognition of his feelings, and which demonstrate a strong empathic understanding of his position. His sister's boyfriend, his sister and his mother are all embraced by Terry's view that there has to be support present to enable the relationships to flourish. This support can override all kinds of other issues which might have prejudiced the relationship, for example the fact that his sister's boyfriend was 'coloured'. This was an issue for Terry, which he acknowledged, but which was dismissed because of the emotional support which his sister's boyfriend gave to him.

Terry is troubled by the lack of understanding demonstrated beyond his intimate circle, and this is probably the reason for his remaining very much at home. This decision has brought him to recognise the importance of learning how to cope with his strong emotional feelings and the difficulties around his brother's behaviour at home. He is aware that he can control his feelings through avoidance and through withdrawal. He has also learnt that self-expression through physical activities such as wrestling and boxing have been beneficial. Despite being troubled by the unfairness of the world, he has created a life at home which is centred on coping with forces which enter his home over which he feels he has some control.

His independent action has moved on from a desire to physically protect his mother, which was the result of a strong attachment to her and a profound fear of what was going to happen to her, to a desire to protect her from the unfairness of a wider society, which he recognises and believes to be true as he observes his mother suffering from unjust treatment. This wider society includes solicitors, neighbours, a brother and church members, who all receive some form of his condemnation. His lack of trust finds expression in his staying at home and his keeping his friends in the setting of school. His disdain for those who discredit his family is whole-hearted.

Terry's emotional bond with his father is broken by his refusal to call him dad any longer. His 'divorce' from his father is something he wants deeply, and is reflected in several mentions of the legal divorce between his mother and father. His severance can only be emotional because contact arrangements are regularly kept; however, this emotional disassociation is crucial to Terry, because it echoes his loyalty to his mother and to the family which supports her. Despite having to spend time with his father, which he says is ok, he is able to hold on to the knowledge that there can be no emotional bonding or closeness because of his father's abusive behaviour. This indicates that Terry has found a degree of autonomy which has developed through his understanding of the controlling core of domestic abuse and violence.

Karl

Karl was 12 years old when he shared his story. Karl's story contains a prevailing sense of loss which touches every part of his life. There is a strong desire for him to find ways of overcoming the losses of his life and he talks about them openly. Having been fearful of his father finding out where they live, he has accepted that there is a real danger of this happening through his father's friends or his brother. He is also fully aware that he had revealed too much to his father during a phone call, and that the repercussions of this were very difficult and caused considerable anxiety. His worries around his father were dealt with by his attempting to put his father completely out of his mind. This was reinforced by a new step-father, who had played an important part in making it easier for the absent father to be forgotten. With a new father figure who provides the family with treats and fun experiences, the loss of his father is softened.

Karl had a deep affection for his dog, and talked in detail about him, and how the dog came to be given away. The sense of injustice is strong, and reveals how Karl views his father's part in adverse and painful experiences. The list of losses is long, but he does not directly blame his father for the loss of his home and garden. However, an impression is drawn and actually expressed of a callous father who does not care about Karl.

The disruption to Karl's life seems all the more unfair and unreasonable when considered against the backdrop of his not having heard or seen any domestic violence. There are issues around the truth of this which will be discussed later on; at this time, his denial of actually witnessing domestic violence is accepted, as is his belief that his father's lack of involvement and idleness around the family was the main reason for the break-up.

Arguments between his mother and father are only very briefly mentioned in the form of an afterthought which almost disappears at the end of his description of life at home with his dad. The fear he feels in relation to his dad seems to have developed through his being aware of his mother's fear, and this indicates a closeness which he does not really express explicitly. He did not really notice a change in his mother after they left except that she was taking more care over her appearance. He talks little about his relationship with his mother, which seems to reflect an increasing lack of concern about her, and a relaxing of the anxiety which had prevailed before going into the refuge. He appears to be content with his life as it has become and talks with pride and confidence that he will have attended four different schools since leaving the family home.

Karl comes across as a sociable person, who seeks out company as a way of dealing with anxiety. He talks about various people in numbers, two or three, as being friends of his mother, and describes his joining in with games and activities with the other children in the refuge. His friend from the refuge, who has remained a friend since his leaving, has a special place as he has been able to stay at his home and he clearly enjoyed his time with him. His relationships within the family are more problematic, particularly his dealings with his older sister. It seems that there has been some tension around their relationship which he sees as having developed during the time when his father was being difficult. When they lived with their father, he could not get on with his sister, and he was quite vague about the reason for this. The problems around the relationship had been carried through to their new life, and there is the feeling that this has been completely accepted by Karl as being something that will probably not change. His concerns are more focused on his younger brother. He is worried about him in that he feels their father would win him over with his gift-buying tactics and then be able to control him so that he would inadvertently divulge where the family was living. This desire to keep their whereabouts secret is a crucial element in Karl's story, and much of his thinking and feelings are a direct result of this desire.

Rose

Rose was 15 years old at the time of her telling her story. She tells her story chronologically, with events of devastating impact swiftly following one after another. It is evident that she has experienced many traumatic changes in her life, particularly in relation to her home, and the almost nomadic existence that she describes is sequentially made sense of through her ability to remember and describe an uninterrupted flow of events. She demonstrates a masterful chronological memory for times, places and events. Her evident grasp of the consequences which proceeded out of the behaviour of the close adults in her life, namely her mum and her step-dad, shows a clear understanding of the reasons for the appalling situation she found herself in. Her enormous pain is described without hesitation. Her guilt around her unkind treatment of her younger sister is stated without reservation. Her story contains a free expression of emotions of every kind, including a remarkable sensitivity to the plight of others.

Alcohol is described by her as being a dreadful component in her life. The whole family had been adversely affected by it to such a degree that it threatened to divide her from her mum, and it seems that alcohol abuse almost succeeded in separating them permanently. This division Rose sees as being both physical and emotional. Alcohol abuse had had a devastatingly negative effect on the behaviour and wellbeing of all the family members. The domestic violence was seen by Rose as also contributing to her severance from her mum, causing a breakdown of affection and attachment. She viewed the consequences as being attributable to the combination of domestic violence and alcohol abuse which led firstly to the disintegration and ultimately to the erosion of her mum's ability to mother her and care for her.

The horrors of her life continued even after the break-up of her mum's marriage to her step-dad. He continued to try and exert control by stalking the family, and it was necessary to start a new life leaving all their possessions behind except for a couple of suitcases. It was essential to leave no trail that could be followed. Their only chance as a family lay in total secrecy in relation to their new whereabouts. This did occur but Rose's troubles did not end as her mum suffered from loneliness and depression once their new life had begun. Rose, who clearly loves her mum, noted that her mum continued to be very unhappy, and that life was grim. Events did take a fortunate turn, however, when her mum decided to get help for herself and for Rose and her sister, as she began to recognise the damage which had been caused to her daughters by their harmful experiences of alcohol abuse and domestic violence.

The support worker who became involved at this stage played a crucial part in rehabilitating the family, specifically working with Rose and her mum individually, strengthening each of them, and assisting them in overcoming the negative effects of the past; these included addiction to alcohol, depression, self-harming, guilt, low self-esteem, loss of attachment and dysfunctional relationships, and which specifically focused on the causes and aftermath of domestic violence. Rose describes her problems with relationships, with schooling and her emotional instability, but recognises that things are now different. She acknowledges her new-formed friendships and her increasing confidence and growing independence. Her sensitivity to the needs of her mum remains, however, despite the damage caused by her apparent rejection of Rose during the most injurious times. Her reproof of her mum is not overtly expressed, and she remains loyal to her mum as she begins to build her own life.

The stories that we have heard here, though skeletal, are precious and need to be seen as such. There may be few opportunities to listen to fragments of young people's lives, and these also must be treasured. As parents, carers, teachers, social workers, support workers and others talk with children and young people, there needs to be an awareness of the value of each piece of their stories which they choose to reveal to adults in their lives, no matter how seemingly insignificant. In situations where a child or young person has been abused through having to live with domestic violence, it must be the case that their stories are taken very seriously, and that every detail is remembered and reflected upon.

The principle of listening to children's stories and acting upon them, in a way which supports them and empowers them, needs to be embraced, and it will ultimately build relationships between young people and adults, and provide a truer understanding of the needs of each young person.

The young people's stories have here begun to unfold. Each has recounted their storied lives, and as the deeper layers of their stories are revealed in subsequent chapters, a depth and richness will be revealed which will be witness of profoundly personal and emotional experiences (Etherington 2004). The panoramic view of each of the stories recounted in this chapter will be examined through a more focused gaze that will allow the gathering of a deeper understanding of each young person's story.

It is crucial not to dismiss anything which is given by a young person. The value of a snippet of a story should be recognised, appreciated and recorded in some way, and this will inevitably produce a feeling within the young person that their stories are being treasured. More of their stories will follow, and many more insights; but the only way this will ever happen is to follow the direction of Mullender (2005) and make every effort to give children and young people a chance to talk.

As Scott talked, it was evident that he had gained a profound understanding of what the support workers had been encouraging him to do, and had used this understanding to modify his behaviour by changing his attitudes.

As Coral talked, it was evident that she had seen herself as being the one to hold everything together, and she had 'held on' successfully until the time came for her mother to step in and sought support for herself and her children.

As Karl talked, it was evident that he had still retained an intense sense of loss, which had remained but which he could manage with strategies which he had naturally developed independently.

As Terry talked, it was evident that he had wanted to protect his mother and that all that had happened had served only to increase this desire. He had not changed this attitude, and remained fiercely protective of her.

As Rose talked, it was evident that in emotional terms she had suffered a great deal, and had needed to blame others for her pain. However, she had learnt through appropriate support to accept the faults of others by seeing them with a greater degree of tolerance and an understanding born of anguish.

It is not hard to assess and interpret stories in this way. The essence of what a young person has experienced may surface spontaneously, and it provides a starting point in knowing what each young person might need. Scott needed to be provided with the tools of support, so that he could make changes to himself and assist others to do the same. Coral needed to be allowed her independence with an understanding that at some point she would recognise that she would do better with help. Karl needed to express himself in lots of ways to find out what worked for him. Terry needed to be encouraged to see that his mother was not his responsibility. Rose needed to know that she could make a decent life for herself with people she chose for herself.

The bare bones may reveal a theme which can act as a guide or starting point in putting together a plan of support for a young person or child. This theme might be what some would call 'a gut feeling', which should not be ignored; but there should always be an attempt to build on or discount this feeling using further reflection and analysis. By doing so, a degree of safeguarding is ensured, in that the support is not based solely on a hunch or on what is believed to be the essence of the need. Rather it is founded on a thorough examination of everything that is contained in the telling of the story, leaving nothing out.

The following chapters of this book reveal my attempt at doing just that.

CHAPTER 2

Voices

Taylor, Gilligan and Sullivan (1995) state that there is a need to learn to listen to voices. The learning process requires the application of complete attention to the voice, followed by a desire to interpret and understand the voice. The meanings underpinning vocal expressions such as emotions, motivations, ideas and understandings can be isolated, but only through the most careful application of analysis and cognitive effort. However, when searching for the essence of a voice, the findings will generally produce a variety of themes which are elusive and hard to pin down. In an effort to understand the character of a voice it may be necessary to 'feel' an overriding projection and distil it into a simple expression such as a 'healing' voice or a 'suffering' voice. Clearly, this can be seen as an over-simplification, but it is still useful in that through sensitively trying to 'feel' the voice of the young person, there is a possibility of hitting upon something which is very significant about the young person at the time.

As young people are given the chance to talk, their voices can provide vital evidence as to what is critical to them and what matters most.

The voices of the young people are now to be heard. When quoting from the words that have been spoken, it was necessary for me to think long and hard about how I was to represent their voices, as there is so much in speech that is difficult, if not impossible, to pin down and express without ambiguity. For example, a silence, a pause or a hesitation could all be expressed by an ellipsis (…), but this cannot and does not convey the fine nuances and meanings contained within each kind of expression. The choice I made was to transpose the spoken words in the simplest way I could devise, but striving at the same time to retain the essence of what was being said. This was done by listening to the recordings countless times, which inevitably led to my retaining in my memory not only what was said, but how it was said. This led to my making an attempt to interpret the emotions which I felt were underlying the spoken words. However, it has to be accepted that my interpretations will be subjective, and as such will need to remain stubbornly illusory and enigmatic. I have not made any claims as to the truthfulness of the representations I have here expressed. However, I hope that the power of the young people's voices will be heard and felt, and that the stories will in some measure contribute to a better understanding of what it means to be experiencing domestic violence as a child or young person.

The voices have been categorised in terms of descriptive words. Such voices as 'healing', 'hurting' and 'knowing' demonstrate what I earlier defined as the essence of each voice. However, these categories are not distinct but fluid. They contain the ability to merge, to dissolve and to surface unexpectedly. Nevertheless, they do assist in creating a useful way into understanding each young person's voice, and as such allow an insight into their idiosyncratic thinking and feeling.

How did the categories come to the surface? It was my interaction with each of the young people which brought the categories to light. We have to get close to the young person without merging with her/him through being drawn in to become an emotional partner. If that was to happen, it would interfere with the interpretative process, and disallow a clear head. The kind of relationship which is needed has been described as 'walking on a knife-edge', in that we need to gain the trust of the young person, and we cannot do that by remaining aloof and distant. Similarly, we need to retain an emotional empathy which young people will recognise and trust. The balancing act does not get easier with practice, as every voice is unique and every story will have different resonances with your own. Being aware of being on a knife-edge does, however, assist in ensuring that the relationship struck up with the young person has a chance of being close enough and yet also distant enough.

Scott's voice

I have chosen three aspects of voice which I describe as Scott's hurting voice, his healing voice and finally, his knowing voice.

I was always harsh towards my family.

Scott recounts his feelings about the way he treated his family. As he reflected upon what he felt as past 'misdemeanours', he recognised the hurt he was passing on to those close to him:

I stayed out of the way for quite a while.

Hurt can and does result in withdrawal from those things which deepen the hurt. Scott withdrew from those who shared his pain. He acknowledged the exchange of painful feelings which added to the weight of abuse. The hurt, which was his alone, remained intact. His motives were not clear to him, but he expressed something which seems to support the idea that he wanted to protect others as well as himself:

Wanted to be my own person... I need time to act like a child.

His feelings of hurt found expression in his worries. The perpetrator was never far away, like a spy who would be interested in what he was saying. Scott lived in fear of being found out:

...would the person using domestic violence and everything, find out...um... about what I was saying and stuff.

The 'stuff' he feared we can only guess at, but it is clear there was a lot of anxiety caused by hurt which found expression in 'I wasn't talking'. Also, Scott was 'staying out of the way'. This can be interpreted in different ways and perhaps the least obvious way is for someone to withhold their voice.

A hurting voice may be an absent, silenced voice. Scott's feelings around hurt were heightened and found expression in what he termed 'weird' experiences. There was something unexplained about what was happening within him, but he recognised that something powerful was happening, because he had possession of unexpected abilities which proved to be of help when he was confronted by violent incidents:

I felt I could (intervene) but there was something holding me back like...fear or something...

...It (domestic violence) was getting really bad...getting really bad, so I knew it was going to happen.

Scott voices his hurt throughout the conversation. It remains almost to the end, as is particularly expressed by the repetition of 'getting really bad'. There were moments when Scott underplayed the hurt, because the hurt was still remembered vividly and powerfully. On seeing his mother hurt, he describes it as 'not very nice'. The words conceal the deep hurt of that time.

Significantly, Scott again uses plain words to describe a time which seems to be the climax of his hurting:

> *It involved the police towards me…(laughs quietly). So I was really silly.*
>
> *I've been in trouble for that…um…I have…*
>
> *I had to get arrested.*

It is significant that there seems to be a contradiction in what Scott is saying and how he is saying it. The use of simple language can conceal deep feelings of hurt and shame. It seems his feelings of silliness conceal a deeper feeling of hurt and pain which results in a revelatory experience, demanding him to respond to those feelings in a completely different way:

> *I decided I'm going to change now.*

This statement ushers in what I am going to call Scott's healing voice. A change takes place which he displays as the beginning of healing, and the dissipation of hurting. I feel I need to stress that Scott's healing voice was a constant presence throughout our time together. I felt its warmth, in Scott's laughter in particular, and I felt its freshness:

> *I've been getting really well…and I think I cope just by staking in there basically…it's getting better…but lately, my attitude has been changing…been growing a lot stronger since then, and try to communicate with people.*

I have used his words from different parts of our conversation, because they demonstrate a growing sense of optimism which comes from healing, and the adverse effects of abuse had begun to dissolve and become less powerful. Scott expresses this healing process:

> *…and lately I've been getting really well.*

These words have caught my eye, because it is an unusual, unexpected turn of phrase. I might have expected him to say that he had been getting *on* really well, but the words he uses point to a change in his health. When we speak of 'getting well' there is an unspoken assumption that all was not well before. Scott voices his belief that he is on the road to recovery, that healing has begun and is continuing.

His awareness of the healing process has led him to consider the reasons for the changes that he feels inside himself. His knowing voice comes into play as he expresses his ideas around what has made a difference to him:

> ...use my experiences and...basically knowledge and everything to help people.

Scott saw the support which was given as providing him with knowledge which he wanted to use to express his own desire to help other people. He recognised the power that this knowledge and understanding gave him:

> I've helped out quite a lot of friends. I persuaded my friend from stopping to self harm their self...we've done a group... I was helping out with some of the people as well... I was doing pretty well.

Scott stated that all this came about because he was able to absorb the support that was given to him, particularly by a teacher who had known him for four years. The absorption meant that he could identify what she was doing for him. He was able to emulate her skills as she supported him:

> I was actually doing her job and stuff. So it felt really good.

It seems clear that the knowledge that he had gained during this period of support had provided the power for him to have an exhilarating experience. This led to other experiences which grew out of the confidence he had gained when he had used his understanding and knowledge to support and assist his friends:

> I think it's my attitude, it's made a difference and also how I think and feel.

Finally, the hurting, healing and knowing voices of Scott have so much to say about each other. There is no clear demarcation between them. The last words quoted demonstrate the complexity of personal stories, and how knowing and feeling are enmeshed, intertwined and tantalisingly difficult to pin down. Being aware of this principle may assist in preventing conclusions which come about without prolonged consideration. As voices are listened to, time and reflection are needed before firm interpretations are attempted.

Healing, hurting and knowing have resonances which provide some insights into where a young person sees themselves, and may be instrumental in understanding what needs to be put into place to assist them to overcome mental health concerns. Young people interviewed for a CAMHS interim report found that every young person valued an approach in which they felt listened to, and were involved in actions taken subsequently (CAMHS 2008). The evidence heartily supports a policy of earlier intervention. There is a need to be sensitive to those aspects of voice which define a troubled young person, and then act sensitively and relatively swiftly in involving the young person in decision-making.

Coral's voice

The themes I have chosen of single voice and multiple voices continue to be at the forefront of thinking. Coral's voice is not easy to categorise, as there are many intricate nuances which cover a spectrum of insights and images which do not easily lend themselves to broad concepts. However, I have chosen to highlight Coral's knowing voice as this I believe is at the centre of her personal power, and it explains much of her story.

The clearest example of the knowledge which Coral shared was her disclosure that she had told her mother to leave:

I was the one who told my mum that we had to get away and tried to make her do it.

She was willing to act upon what she knew, and presented to her mother the knowledge that she possessed, with the added action of 'making' her mother behave in such a way as to support her daughter's knowledge. Coral exhibits enormous confidence in the knowledge she has acquired. This confidence is made manifest by her making her mother act in accord with what she knew to be right. Coral displays this kind of confidence in her recognising the concerns of her best friend. Despite the relative shortness of their friendship, she states:

I can talk to her about nearly everything... I say to her all the time that if she needs to talk she can...

The dual concepts of 'talking' and 'everything' remain central and connected in Coral's thinking. One has a kind of dependence on the other and she embraces the idea that they are intimately intertwined and should be so:

Now that it's all out and I've told everything, I feel that it's always going to be there but I can kind of move on...

Earlier she had believed that talking to just her mum was all she needed to do, but she recognised her mother's observation that this was not sufficient:

> ...she thinks that I didn't talk to her about everything.

In consequence, a support worker had been working with her and her brother while they were in the refuge, and Coral accepted this development and recognised the significance of talking to him about things which were too sensitive for her mother:

> I was scared I would make her upset...

The consequences of knowledge of personal convictions and feelings are clearly visible in Coral's view of her situation:

> I was scared it might make her want to take him back again.

She is fully aware that her knowledge provides the means to destroy what she sees as an improving situation, and freely states that these consequences were at the forefront of her thinking. She would do nothing to jeopardise the overall deeply held conviction that her mother, herself and her brothers would all be better off away from the father. With the recognition that once everything had been acknowledged and brought out into the open through talking about it, she knew that she could move on, and has been able to see that her relationship with her father will probably never change:

> He changed for like two days and then he was back to his normal self. So I just knew it was all an act. He wasn't going to change.

> He was there to help and...he wasn't like my dad... I know there's other people out there that can help and that they're not just there to ruin our life...

> I would...just listen to Eminem...and I used to wish that dad would be just like that with me...but obviously he wasn't.

> I love my dad but I just knew that it was the right thing (to leave).

Acknowledging the rightness of a course despite strong feelings which would have the power to deviate her from that course, she voiced her belief that there was always the possibility of being persuaded not to follow the right course:

> She'd left before and gone back to him. I knew this had to be the last time.

In her eyes, it was her mother's last chance to leave, and there could be no going back. Coral retrospectively was able to imagine the circumstances which precluded the possibility of going back. There was, for her, no other way. She knew with a certainty born of her experiences which had left an indelible mark; through these experiences, she had created a picture of her life, a family image without her father. This image had become a reality in that she had severed contact with her father after 'a huge argument, a lot of crying and screaming in the middle of the street'.

The public nature of this severance strengthened her perception of what she had imagined. She had created a better life without her father, and she states this simply.

> *I feel that...we might not have as much stuff as what everyone else does...but I'm happy like with what we do have...'cos we started with nothing.*

Her picture, her image of what she had hoped for, had not depended upon 'stuff', but she wanted above everything to know that her mother was alright:

> *...I hated seeing her and hearing it (domestic violence).*

Her image of 'getting away' was based on the eradication of painful, sensory and emotional experiences; this done, Coral has found happiness because the hatred, which had accompanied her previous life, had now become a distant memory.

Interestingly, Coral's knowing voice is very much centred on her relationship with her mother. The most powerful emotion expressed was in relation to her mother. There is only one repetition throughout the interview, which is about her and her mother:

> *We have a very good relationship...*

> *We have a really good relationship.*

The significance of the relationship cannot be overestimated. A lot of knowledge is accrued around her mother, and is dependent upon Coral's vision of their relationship which has as a component an intriguing sharing of power, which shifts and fluctuates according to circumstances:

> *I wanted to help her...*

> *I know it was hard for her.*

> *My mum was trying to be like a mum and dad for me...*

I stopped joining in with her…just left her.

These statements indicate changes in the exercising of power within their relationship. There is a poignancy to 'just left her' which strikes at the heart of what Coral is trying to express. Her decision to intercede and then to withdraw contains a degree of matter of factuality which may conceal feelings of powerlessness which emanate from situations where the only way empowerment can occur is through acting and then retreating. The vision of this young girl having to leave her mother to face her attacker alone arouses our compassion. Her words echo this miserable situation:

She would always reassure me…but I did still feel guilty.

The power sharing between mother and daughter ebbed and flowed. Coral's confidence has seemingly developed from her recognition of forces over which she has some control, and this has made her into a powerful partner, in some instances holding precedence over her mother. She knows she has a controlling influence, which has probably accumulated because of the strains and stresses of living with abuse. It would seem likely that in the absence of a supportive husband, the mother would turn more and more to a daughter who is supportive and helpful. They would clear up the house together, Coral would stay with the boys when things were kicking off, and it was clear that Coral sided with her mother in her actions, support and words.

The relationship tends to sound like a friendship with some unspoken boundaries which were all about personal safety. However, the reassuring voice is definitely a mother's voice, her mother's voice, one which wishes to nurture, protect and encourage her. The mother in Coral's eyes is 'good', and there is a feeling that this is compounded by the mother first taking the blame for Coral's wayward actions, and second, the recognition that the domestic violence was not either's fault. All these elements compounded the ties between mother and daughter, which hold, despite the tremendous shifting of their lives and the resultant pressure brought about by these shifts and changes.

In conclusion, Coral's knowing voice confidently strikes out at what is unacceptable. There is no room for hesitancy, and very little time for sympathy. The correctness of her evaluation of their circumstances has been proved, she knows, by the outcome of their actions based upon her evaluation. This has resulted in a voice which is both self-assured and courageous. It is quietly so, however, because Coral does not see her present life in terms of her own success. More than that, she is sensitive to the positions held by others and expresses this in relation to her friend:

...but I think she's worried.

This awareness has developed through the recognition of the value of her own experiences and those of other people, and a significant sensitivity which is present within her relationships. In this way a voice which is defined may demonstrate a strong sense of identity, and this can be the foundation of further enquiry and questioning. This supports research carried out by Ecclestone and Hayes (2009) which stressed the critical need to focus on positive psychology in relation to wellbeing. So much of the past has been focused on negative aspects and what has gone wrong, rather than on a model of a human being which possesses positive features. Coral's voice clearly demonstrates this important principle, and is, I believe, a guide to how we need to approach discerning the quality of an individual's voice.

Terry's voice

Terry revealed himself to be highly energised and clear in relation to his thinking. There seemed very little room for doubt in his expressions, and this is why I began by choosing to analyse and interpret what I felt as being his strident voice; however, I think that there are connotations to 'strident' which are not entirely positive, and although his voice is distinctive, there remains a sensitivity and emotionality which 'strident' does not describe. Much of what Terry describes contains a 'troubled' dimension in that there is a clear questioning of moral positions in relation to what constitutes acceptable and unacceptable behaviour towards others:

They talk to me, I just don't to them 'cos I really get annoyed. I don't see the point.

His observation that other people have the capacity to annoy him, and that there is no point in developing relationships with these people, reflects his position that his feelings should be a strong indicator of where he stands. It is interesting that the 'point' has probably been defined in some way, in order for Terry to have rejected it. He had to know about the point in the first place, if he was to consciously disregard it:

...he tries to start a fight... I just push him over. I don't see the point of hitting him...

His brother does not appear to create such an emotive response from him, and he is able to respond in what he sees as an acceptable way, using various means to avoid the possibility of his feelings becoming his master. His moral position seems to echo the degree of emotional commitment to the person involved.

He (dad) pretended he didn't know her (his daughter) but thought it was a joke but it wasn't funny...if I told her she really wouldn't like it, and she would cry and I don't want to see her cry...

His decision to keep secret something which he saw as harming the happiness of someone he loved is a powerful testimony of his desire to add to their emotional wellbeing. An acceptable moral position, he believes, is dependent upon the emotional investment made. Where the attachment is slight, there is 'no point' in trying to overcome negative emotions, and build something stronger. Similarly, where the emotional investment is great, there is every point in doing everything you can to build that relationship into something even stronger.

This moral position is reflected in his attitudes to various people outside the close confines of his immediate family. In ethical terms, he sees many people as being untrustworthy, who are mainly motivated by selfishness, greed, dishonesty or unkindness:

Even though he (dad) lies all the time.

He (older brother) left us to deal with it (domestic violence).

My dad didn't have any money no more, so he (older brother) didn't need him anymore.

I was naughty one lesson and he (teacher) just hated me since then.

He'll (dad) start crying but then everyone will be on his side...it gets on my nerves...

I don't like solicitors anymore. They're just in it for the money.

There is a strong degree of outrage which Terry exhibits both in his responses to these people, and in the expressions of indignation which he voices privately. His attitudes to those whom he sees as untrustworthy are strongly held, but not entirely rigid and set in stone:

I never used to have respect for coloured people... I used to be scared...they (the news) always say it's always the black people but it's not.

A seemingly trustworthy source, the news, as experienced by Terry, has been overturned by an intimate knowledge which has completely changed Terry's view. His relationship with his sister's boyfriend, seemingly founded on his love for his sister, has become an immensely important part of Terry's life:

My sister calls every day... I love my sister, she's great and her boyfriend. He's cool.

Linking associations by affection or disassociations by distrust is brought about by the fear of dreadful consequences of having people close to you who will stop at nothing to gain control:

My mum was being sick...every time she went to the toilet...crying nearly every second of the day... I don't want to see her like that again...she'll be safe 'cos I know that I can defend her... I used to push him away and everything...but if I didn't do it and my mum would get really hurt and she was crying on the floor...she was really hurt... I used to cry 'cos I thought I could have stopped that but I didn't...

The anguish of Terry is clearly felt, and provides a fuller understanding of why he has taken his particular moral ground which does not allow another person the possibility of closeness to him, with an associated respect, unless they have been introduced by a trusted family member, as in the case of his sister's boyfriend, or have proved themselves to be emotionally supportive, as in the case of the domestic violence support worker. The emotional element of any kind of relationship is the determining factor for Terry.

The isolation created by domestic violence is something which Terry describes in stark detail:

My mum never went to town. She was always at home...the only place that she went which was not home was Tescos or my nan's...

I don't go out anymore...I haven't got many friends in that area...I'm just scared for my mum.

The bleakness of his life and his mother's still influences every part of his life. Despite his mum being 'a lot better now', he finds he has to respond to a deeply embedded desire to protect her, even though he knows he is a 'teenager' and should have his own life. The dangers of 'another man' are keenly felt and provide the reason for his isolation, as he stays home because he knows that he can 'defend her'.

There does seem to be a single word that I can use to describe Terry's voice. It is an 'emotive' voice. It is troubled, indignant, loving, fearful and brave...a voice that remains with the listener long after the words have been spoken. A quality of a voice may be prevalent to such a point that it is difficult to decipher any other tones. It will necessitate a very sensitive approach in order to achieve a full understanding of the voice. Possibly Terry's voice demonstrates the link between mothers traumatised by domestic violence and their avoidance of interaction with and restricted capacity to respond to their children's emotional and physical needs (Lieberman 2004). As a troubled voice is heard it would be necessary to reflect on the impact of a mother's limited emotional availability, and the consequences of this.

Karl's voice

Karl's voice is characterised by the feeling that he is going through a transitional phase which has a lot to do with the almost complete lack of continuity and common factors between his past life and the present. It appears that the only cohesive factor has been his mother. Everything else had changed or been lost. Karl is very selective about what he remembers from the past. Some things are described quite readily because they occurred 'ages before we left'. Other experiences, more recent and more intense, are 'just ignored'.

The emptiness of Karl's life is expressed in various ways. His sense of loss is often described in covert terms. He does not wish to admit that the garden and his bike have gone, and that if his father had made a positive contribution to the family, they might still be together:

We had a really nice garden...

...he said my bike rusted away in the garage...

(Mum decided to leave) because he (dad) never did anything.

Each statement conceals a longing for things to have been different, his wish for his garden and his bike, and his wish for his father to have behaved differently. He seems to express this longing in a way which is not seeking sympathy. The hurt contained in these statements is not allowed to surface. The statements appear to be devoid of underlying emotion, and are simple observations of what has happened. There is some evidence of grief, however, contained in his story which is centred around his dogs:

...we had a dog when I was born which ran away and then I had my own dog... I had my own which was a Labrador and I called it —, and it could jump a seven foot fence...we gave it to the police...we never got its injections because he (dad) wouldn't let us... I was like really annoyed and that... I didn't like it when my other dog ran away.

The anger which Karl felt was compounded by his father's part in the loss of his 'own' dog, which echoed his feelings at the loss of the other dog. His association between the two experiences demonstrates his fondness towards both dogs, and the emptiness which ensued when they were both lost to him. His loss was compounded, and the first reaction to grief, that of anger, was the result. His anger is expressed in relation to his father not returning his possessions when he had made an arrangement to do so. Karl's grieving is almost hidden by his 'coolness' and calmness. His tone is one of indifference, but I interpret this as a stance which Karl assumes because it helps him cope with his feelings:

...he said he was going to give it all (our stuff) to my auntie... When my auntie went to meet him to get the stuff...um...he didn't have any...he wasn't even there.

Karl gives little away except annoyance at what his father had done. The disappointment he must have felt must have been acute.

Karl is confused and bewildered by his new home. He is displaced in an emotional sense as well as in a physical sense:

I didn't really know because I'd never heard anything about it. I never even knew it existed.

There is a strong feeling that he has accepted this condition because of the overriding fear of his father finding out their whereabouts. Their safety requires some form of sacrifice, and Karl is more than ready to accept this. Despite his confusion, the displacement has been accepted and tolerated by him.

In conclusion, the transition of Karl is evident in his quiet acceptance of his mother's new boyfriend or, as he corrects himself, husband.

A characteristic of accepting a new life can be acquiescence; there is no sign of rebellion or a feeling of disquiet with the way his new life is going. There is a feeling that Karl is satisfied for the present. His only fear is centred on his father, who has proved untrustworthy and volatile:

> ...I know how to control my anger, not be like, well, my dad was like.

As Karl experiences this crucial transition, he has evolved a tactic which has involved forgetting his father as much as he could and disassociating himself from his previous life. His voice is strangely unemotional as he describes the evolution of his new life.

His search for peace and an untroubled life has led him to a place which feels acceptable:

> I think like it's (family) improved a lot.

Karl's 'accepting' voice has been affected by the domestic violence, but he is gaining strength and confidence as he finds some emotional and physical security in his new life. A voice which demonstrates a particular longing or willingness to conform to a specific way of thinking can be challenging to understand fully, because the voice hides many facets of the person, and it may be very difficult for the listener to find a way through what feels like barriers to understanding. However, Rutter (2004) encourages a view of support which needs to remain consistent, particularly when applied to children and young people who have experienced considerable losses, and will need assistance to 'accept' their new lives and situations.

Rose's voice

Rose's story describes with intensity the close and intimate relationships which surround her, but remains silent for the most part in relation to a broader context, that of the community which she inhabits. Her voice is for the most part concerned with and fixed upon personal issues and lingers on private and intensely sensitive concerns. Her public voice has a comparatively brief focus on school, social care professionals and the Council with no other reference to the wider community:

> ...we was put into B and B by the Council... The Council said to us we have just to up and go and we had to leave everything behind...

Rose expresses concerns about the power wielded by public authority to make decisions which have dreadful repercussions, and which seemingly are made with little empathic thought for those involved. The loss of all their possessions except for a few clothes indicates an apparent callous disregard on the part of the authorities for the consequences of their actions, which resulted in a victim of harassment and stalking by a previous violent partner being victimised further. There is so much of Rose's story that indicates an almost total lack of emotional, financial and advisory support which should be expected as the fundamental right of all victims of domestic violence.

It is for this reason that her voice exemplifies what it means to be a survivor. The essence of her story is that despite things going from bad to worse, and despite the inability of anyone to recognise that Rose's family was suffering from an appalling series of crises, which required a package of supportive interventions to help them, the family survived. It is true that a support worker did appear on the scene, but only at the mother's invitation when it seems that their lives could not have got much worse:

> *Mum was so depressed...she just wanted to drink all the time... I was going through a stage of self-harming...*

It seems that not at any point did a statutory or voluntary agency provide support or advice. Rose and her mum and sister had had to fend for themselves. There is a sense that the pressures made upon the family as a whole to be self-reliant and not in any way dependent upon outside services had in some measure caused each member of the family to find her own solutions:

> *I got bullied at school... So I went to live with my nan... I had to come back... and finish school here.*

> *I tried to do everything I could so that my mum wouldn't get beaten up.*

> *I did speak to one of my friends...*

Challenges were apparently met individually and solutions carved out without any explanation as to how the decisions were reached within the family. This individualistic way of dealing with hardship and crisis is mirrored by Rose's definition of what it was that changed her life into one that had a share of happiness:

I was allowed to be me for once... I don't care what anyone else thinks as long as I'm happy and as long as my mum's happy... I'm going to be there to support her (mum) but as the child at the same time...

Rose is absolutely clear in how she sees herself, and how her identity has a bearing on her responsibilities. Being 'me' has an integrity which seems to have grown from the imposition of having to survive alone and unsupported. The damage she felt she needed to inflict upon herself was cursory:

...slitting my wrists and things like that...it wasn't properly done or nothing. It was just to get attention, back then...

To be a survivor, there is, in one sense of its definition, the possibility that others have died. A widow survives her husband. An orphan survives her parents. Rose remains alive, whilst death of a kind had touched all those around her. Each tragic character exhibits a withdrawal, a loss or a rejection of human relationships. Rose's mum turns to alcohol for solace. Rose tries to erase the person nearest her, her sister:

...when we were left alone, I tipped Coke over her (my sister's) head... 'You can't touch my things... You go over there, just leave me alone.'

It appeared that Rose, her mum and her sister were each treading their own single path, intent on their own survival. The paths overlapped at only one point apparently, when the support worker spent time with Rose and her mum, but there is a feeling that this did not occur simultaneously. The support of one had to be quite different from that with the other:

...he said it was time for my mum to be the mum and me to be the teenager...

Rose's path has remained separate from her sister. Her relationship seems to revolve around making amends for her earlier rejection of her:

I'm trying to make up for it now...'cos like I try to be there for her now.

Later she admits that she goes out more and more with her friends:

I feel it's ok for me to do my own thing now...as soon as I'm old enough I can leave...

The solitary path has broadened, but at the time of telling her story, Rose was not allowing those who had suffered with her to join her, as she exercised her new-found growing confidence. Perhaps the unaided existence of her previous life had in some measure contributed to her self-sufficiency and had demanded a greater degree of self-government; she had become abnormally unconnected from her family through circumstance. Now she has become disconnected through choice. Connections are formed through conjoining and adhesion. There seems to have been very little attempt at uniting the family by Rose's mum, and no apparent 'glue' applied by her to the relationships. So, Rose had slipped away into a world of her own making, with just an occasional, brief pang of guilt over leaving her mum, which she easily dismisses:

> I've kind of pushed my mum out, which makes me feel really bad sometimes... but then I...feel like when my mum had all that time to have...to have all the time with me but she never took it...she pushed me out...so I'm not trying to get back at her or nothing but I feel it's ok for me to do my own thing.

Accompanying the pang of guilt there is a reference to a moral code which allows Rose to do what she is doing. She is not getting back at her mum. Her life experiences have taught her that it's ok for her to take control of her life, even if it means 'pushing' her mum out.

Rose's 'survivor' voice prevails as one of optimism but also acceptance of the damaging impact of the past. There is a sense that she has remained distant from the source of her suffering, which has allowed her to embrace a positive demeanour in all her relationships. The self-imposed distancing from those who possess painful associations has seemingly allowed Rose the breathing space to develop her own identity, without unduly hurting other people's feelings. She believes she is justified in what she is doing. She has to look out for herself now. This idea holds precedence over all others, as her life moves forward and expands in entirely new directions, with hardly a backward glance.

Her voice is confident and demonstrates the comfortable position which Rose has now established. The past does not hold any terrors now. Perhaps this is why she is able to talk about it with such ease, with such fluidity and eloquence. A voice which is very audible is refreshing and comforting. It is listened to with ease, and appears to hold no dangers. It is easy possibly to get drawn into becoming complacent, and lose sight of the need for rigour and a questioning attitude. There is a need to consider how the journey of a young person possessing a voice of confidence and self-reliance came about. If we are able to discern the answer to that, it may well provide some ideas about how to foster greater resilience in others. The capacity of some to overcome disadvantage and to 'bounce back' from adversity needs to be studied and understood. The relationships we develop with young people play a pivotal role in promoting resilience amongst those who have experienced disadvantage (Spratt *et al.* 2010).

Others' voices

What is so important that the voices of children and young people should be understood, analysed and recorded? Why should those of us who are willing to listen and take note act upon what we are told? What evidence is there to support the crucial nature of listening to the voices of children and young people?

The voices we have heard are the voices of empowered people (Fine 1992), because voices heard are intrinsically empowered. This empowerment is fundamental to the UN Convention on the Rights of the Child, which states that due weight needs to be given to the views of children and young people (Article 12) and that the overarching vision should be the empowerment of children. Allowing them the opportunity, permission (Hester, Pearson and Harwin 2007) and space to speak is fundamental to our understanding of what constitutes the rights of any individual.

Unfortunately, there have been many who have used discouraging arguments to dissuade those who would embrace this philosophy, and have primarily argued that children and young people do not have the capacity, for a variety of reasons, to provide useful insights into areas of their lives. Also, traditionally repressed voices, such as those of children and young people, have been silenced and subordinated with the view that they are not part of dominant discourses, and, as such, should remain hidden as they are of little consequence.

Therefore, until relatively recently, listening to children's voices and facilitating their exposure has not always been generally embraced by those who come into regular contact with them. However, the idea of participation, resulting in the full involvement of young people in services, education and decision-making, has grown in prevalence and this work supports the idea of a continuation and an expansion of this practice.

Nevertheless, it has been consistently stated in various ways that we must seek to understand the child's point of view. This is developed further with the direction, as was stated earlier, that we should learn to listen to their voices (Taylor *et al.* 1995). Not only that, but we should listen and then take their views seriously (Newell 2000). Along with this is the encouragement to do all these things through direct contact with them (ibid.).

Trying to understand the child's point of view is central to working with children and young people. By expressing themselves through their voices, they are empowered, they are enabled to make sense of what has happened, and by telling their stories they enter a place where their life story is reaffirmed and modification of its living is possible. This development of a life through the voicing of a story is what Kiesinger (1998) describes as a process which involves thinking, feeling and remembering, and giving voice to deeper meanings and mysteries.

In order for this to happen, clearly, there needs to be a capacity to achieve a situation where a child or young person will feel confident enough to voice their stories. Methods need to be employed which are most likely to help them express themselves. The skill and experience required to provide the necessary methods which support and encourage young people to talk can be developed and understood through training about domestic violence and a deep commitment to children and young people.

My hope is that by sharing my analysis of the young people's voices, it will encourage all of us to listen with a more concentrated mind and heart, and allow us to perceive the essence of the young person in a way which is reflected in her or his voice. I would not be so rash as to say that when we become occupied in this way then the result will always be entirely trustworthy, remembering the 'knife-edge' that we are walking as we engage with young people. We have to recognise our own subjectivity in this kind of endeavour, and look to continue to piece together, as we come into contact with each young person, a view which is supported by further evidence. This is why the listening has to continue with ongoing deliberation, and the gathering of further conceptualisations and ideas has to be pursued.

CHAPTER 3

Emotional Journeys

Emotionality: locating the feeling voice

Emotional elements associated with each of the young people's voices have already surfaced, but in a broad, indistinct kind of way. As I listened to their stories over and over again, I became aware of streams of emotionality which were distinct and could be discerned with clarity. There were two main streams which flowed one into another, intermingling and fusing, revealing complex forms of emotionality.

The feelings expressed by the young people were varied, convergent and numerous. However, it became apparent that some were indicative of suffering, whilst others were pointing towards declarations founded on healing and recuperation. In this way, two broad ideas had surfaced within the category of 'feeling', which provided the basis for the following descriptions, those of the suffering voice and the healing voice.

As we consider the suffering and healing of children and young people, and how we can recognise these elements of their lives through listening carefully to their voices, I hope that the voices here recorded will in some way facilitate the deserving attention and increase the ability of the reader in seeking to understand the feelings of other young people. It has been estimated that 20 per cent of children and young people in this country experience mental health problems which broadly encompass emotional and behavioural difficulties (Loades and Mastroyannopoulou 2010). The prevalence of these problems must surely encourage and also prevail upon us to learn how to recognise them. It is my desire to enable others to do what I have sought to do, which is to reach a deeper understanding of what it means to suffer and to heal, after being exposed to damaging experiences such as domestic violence. Emotional difficulties associated with suffering are dwelled upon, and the need to discover those elements of young people's lives which alleviate mental and emotional problems has been at the forefront of my thinking.

The empathy I felt as I immersed myself in the voices of a few valiant young people has, I have discovered, in some measure assisted me in my work with others, as I have become more conscious of the depths inherent in the telling of a human story, and the complexity of human emotion. I hope that this can be achieved by others who share in my desire to understand and support young people, and who will gain deeper insights into suffering and healing associated with domestic violence and abuse.

The five young people are each individuals, who expose their innermost feelings, and who remain unique and utterly distinct. As we consider the lives of each of these young people, we recognise the singularity of each of them, and how we must beware of making generalisations; each child and young person has a distinct and special identity which must remain central to our thinking.

Let us follow each of the young people's journeys with complete respect, remembering that each path traced is of equal value and worth.

Disempowering emotionality and abuse: locating the suffering voice

Some individuals survive violence and suffering whilst others do not (Mananzan *et al.* 1996). However, 'the pain permeates the being of all women' (Ackermann 1996), and it follows that the pain felt by children and young people also penetrates all who care about them. Here the aim is to honour those who have not survived (ibid.) and to hold in high esteem those who have only just begun the journey from debilitating emotions born of suffering to empowering, humanising emotions which indicate the arrival at a more desirable destination. The view here is that those whose struggles are far from over are no less worthy than those who have seemingly arrived and survived. It is also the view held that the journey spoken of has an intrinsic worth in every respect and that disempowering emotions possess a complexity and interrelatedness which may conceal their value as motivators and strengtheners. However, these emotions are generally accompanied by anguish.

With a deep sense of the reflective and ethical considerations which must be employed whilst analysing and interpreting such emotions felt by the young people, that have tended to disempower them and exacerbate their suffering and accompanying pain, every effort has been made to sensitively examine these feelings. There is the recognition that all facets of emotionality should be valued, as an intrinsic part of human experience. To honour all the feelings of the young people in all their complexity is an overriding principle which is consistently adhered to throughout this analysis. As Boler encourages, the aim here is to '"recuperate" emotions from their shunned status and reclaim them in new ways' (1999, p.xxiv).

The disempowering emotions which surfaced from the young people's stories, and which are focused upon in this chapter, are fearfulness, aggressiveness and bitterness.

Fearfulness

When it first started happening, when — started beating up my mum, it was more like I was really scared, scared mostly because like I was only little and just didn't know why… (Rose)

The rawness of Rose's reaction as a 'little' child, the intensity of those feelings of being 'scared, scared' indicate a powerful mixture of incomprehension and shock. As young as she was, she was now able to isolate her initial reaction to abuse, with the knowledge that her feelings would change and adjust, and she would respond differently as she grew more mature. The narrowness and intensity of her early response, Rachman argues, is due to the power and force of the threat and there may be 'enhanced perceptual sensitivity and even distortion' (1998, p.27). As the abuse continued, Rose's feelings became more complex as she recognised a pervading fearful guilt which was the result of imposed blame. Her step-father convicted Rose of being responsible for the abuse, and so she accepted the blame and the punishment:

I tried to do everything I could so that my mum wouldn't get beaten up…so it was like a case of doing the right thing at that point.

Acknowledging the blame required that Rose took responsibility for her fearfulness. The perpetrator is distanced and becomes a remote, almost unidentifiable, entity. Fear is seen as self-inflicted and because fear requires an attempt to avoid or escape the threat (Rachman 1998), Rose has to do 'the right thing' and take total responsibility. It is her only means of escape.

FEARFULNESS AND GUILT

Feelings of guilt are associated with feelings of anxiety and fear (McKeating 1970). Coral remembered the time when she was 'not happy at all', adding that her mother would be blamed if she did anything wrong. Guilt for her was an easy progression as she fearfully tried to deal with her direct witnessing of the violence. Any intervention she had tried had 'made everything worse', and so she 'had just left her (her mother)'. The agony of abandoning the closest person to her, the only one she was able to talk to, her mother, must have been acute. Despite her mother's efforts in reassuring Coral, she did still feel guilty. The guilt, the shame and the fear became a terrible burden.

This is echoed by Rose, who viewed herself as an object of contempt and shame. Lewis and Granic describe this emotional state as 'a sudden loss of control, coupled with a heightened state of self awareness' (2000, p.24). There were repeated experiences of abuse which led to an arousal of 'cognitive themes of abandonment and worthlessness coupled with hopelessness and guilt' (ibid., p.378). Rose fell to this awful state as she considered suicide:

> I used to write things down like I wish I was dead and things like that… I just wished that I weren't around most of the time…

As the feelings of fear were activated, Rose appears to have experienced a decline in her ability to view herself without a sense of shame. As fearfulness took hold, she recognised later that she had reached a place where depression had taken hold and she needed to find ways of concealing the fear from others and even from herself:

> …I just buried myself into my school work and just pretend what was going on at home weren't really happening.

Her effort to entirely conceal her fear and guilt was almost completely successful. However, her fear that anyone would get to know about the abuse was overridden, because of a stronger feeling that it was emotionally crucial and safe for her to confide in someone. She knew this when she decided to tell a friend what was happening:

> It was kind of good 'cos me, me and her, we could relate quite…how can I put it? It was just nice to know someone was there… It was like I could talk and not be frightened of it going anywhere because she knew what I was going through.

Rose found a state of 'not being frightened' which was simply 'good' and 'nice', and allowed her to feel the warmth of empathy. This emotional change is echoed later by Rose as she revealed the palliative 'relief' which formed a 'release' for her when her mother admitted her part in the pain:

> ...she does now say I have put you through a lot and things like that, and she does feel like bad for what she's put me and my sister through.

Circumstances appear to have an important bearing on whether or not fear can be released and concealment challenged. The context for Rose was dependent on feeling safe, so that she felt that the threat had been adequately removed. As avoidance and escape from threats are the primary reactions (Rachman 1998, p.6), it would appear that something deeper had occurred which enabled Rose to share her fears.

FEARFULNESS AND CONCEALMENT

Coral succeeded in completely concealing her pain from the outside world:

> I thought I'd speak to my mum, and I didn't think I needed to speak to anyone else.

Later, however, in the refuge, her mother challenged Coral's dependence on her, and acknowledged her daughter's need to talk to someone else:

> ...she thinks that I didn't talk to her about everything.

Coral agreed that this was the case:

> I didn't want always to talk about it because I was scared I would make her upset and I was scared...

Talking to her mother heightened her fearfulness, and so avoidance and concealment were used to manage the situation. However, the refuge did provide a circumstance for change when she was introduced to a support worker:

> I think that really helped me because I was keeping a lot of stuff inside and I didn't really want to talk to anyone about it... Just knowing that he (support worker) was there to help and that he wasn't like my dad...

Coral had overcome her fearfulness which had previously prevailed, through her recognition that there existed 'other people **out there** that can help' (emphasis added).

Rachman describes Rose and Coral's concealment of their suffering as 'repression', and with the blocking of intolerable memories which arise from intolerable levels of anxiety there comes an associated blocking of the present suffering (1998, p.49). Rose does, however, allow a small conduit through the blocking, which offers her the possibility of 'not being frightened', as she shares experiences with a friend who understood in the fullest sense. Her friend also knew what it was like to be fearful, and they were able to 'kind of relate really well'.

Coral's effort to conceal what was happening was to conceal herself in her room:

Most of the time I would just sit in my room...

Otherwise she conveys a compulsive effort to carry on, independent and autonomous:

I didn't think I needed to speak to anyone.

I just got on with my work and...did things I had to.

This state of being is due in part to fear being acquired by conditioning or other learning (Rachman 1998). If being fearful is an aspect of your life which has been learnt, then it seems probable that cognitive means are employed to manage fears. There is a 'need to exert a great deal of effort in an attempt to control fear and anxiety by cognitive means because these emotions can be so dominating' (ibid., p.52). Coral and Rose used 'work' and 'writing' to handle their fear, employing activities which require effort and mental application at the time of their greatest pain.

MANAGING FEARFULNESS

Rose specifically states that her writing was a 'release' and a 'comfort'. The conduit through the blocking of the suffering appears to be the mental absorption. As Coral listened to Eminem, she considered the differences between the artist and her father. The thoughtfulness of her isolation appears to have determined her release and comfort. As the intellect and imagination were engaged, there followed a means of overcoming fear which diverted consciousness and released pain.

Worrying may be seen as a symptom of fearfulness. Here, cognitive processes may be recognised as truly debilitating. Impairment caused by worries and the distortions which may inherently accompany worries (Rachman 1998, p.27) may both exist:

I'm still worried about him (dad) finding out where we live.

How long is it since you actually left?

About three or four years ago. (Karl)

Yes, I always do (worry about mum). That's why I don't go out anymore. (Terry)

The impact of fear can be seen in seemingly illogical concerns which traverse time and place. Terry cannot remove himself from his mother, because the threat is perceived as real and strong still. Karl views his father as a continuing threat, despite the passing of 'three or four years'. Managing fear consumes so much of a young person's existence that it appears to override much of what is seen as typical and logical thought.

Management seems to produce unreal and abnormal reactions, and fears may be held on to because they possess so much power.

FEAR AND ANXIETY

Fears and anxieties may be defined differently. Whereas fears may have a specific focus, anxiety may be felt without a clear idea of the cause. Fear may be seen to decline once a threat has been removed, whilst anxiety remains persistent, prolonged and puzzling (Rachman 1998). The pervasive and persistent uneasiness which characterises anxiety can often follow fear (ibid., p.6). However, the young people do recognise the source of their worries. The intensity of their feelings, surrounded as they have been by abuse of the cruellest kind, has resulted in a prolonged and slow diffusing of the fear. Despite the removal of the fear-inducing threats, in that they are no longer in direct contact with the perpetrators, these young people remain open to the possibility of the return of the threat so their worries remain.

The thought processes which accompany fear-induced worrying were not fully perceived or expressed by Scott. His experience of worry was based on him having frightening premonitions of when the abuse was going to happen and he experienced a mix of emotions:

Not very happy...worried...miserable...angry.

The power of the disempowering emotions prevented him from responding or doing anything when he knew the abuse was going to start:

I felt I could (do something) but there was something holding me back like... fear or something.

Fearfulness requires a response which embodies avoidance. However, when a relationship is threatened or endangered, the emotional response is anxiety and anger (Bowlby 1988). 'A feature of attachment behaviour is the intensity of emotion that accompanies it. If it is threatened there is jealousy, anxiety and anger' (ibid., p.79).

Scott goes on to describe the times when he stepped in to help his mother:

Sometimes I actually got in the argument I tried to stop it and...

Clearly on these occasions the fear which had held him back before was now replaced by another emotion, perhaps anger. As the focus at this time is on the fearful voice, it is interesting to note that fear did not prevail. Bowlby reflects that anger and anxiety are both from the same etymological root (1998, p.80). It appears that one emotion may be interchangeable with the other, that conversion from one to the other does occur and that the crossover is easily facilitated.

The young people who express their fearfulness less appear to express their anger more. This idea is supported by Rachman who describes fear as 'a combination of tension and unpleasant anticipation' (1998, p.2). This definition seems to point to the idea that contained within fear there is a combustible element based on 'tension', which might get inflamed into anger. As Scott tried to stop his 'mum getting hurt' the anger he felt was turned on him:

I usually got shouted at or threatened...

This example is given here because it demonstrates a metamorphic, mutating quality contained within fear.

Fearful emotions do dissipate, however, and Coral describes this process in relation to the fear that she had had in the past that her mother would go back to her father. This was an intense feeling for her because she had seen her mother return more than once. She was tense and apprehensive:

I was scared it (my talking to mum) might make her want to take him back again.

The process of removing her fear was grounded in observing her mother's actions and applying her knowledge of her mother in shaping her conclusions:

...we missed dad so mum started to try and get us to have contact with him. So she would drop us off...but then he would always just like get in the car with her...when she knew that wasn't right because she was bringing us there to see him...she didn't want to see him. So in the end she stopped doing that...but I think that she realised that she couldn't take him back no matter what.

Coral's worries were gone. The specific fear had dispersed. It had been observed by her that her mother had at last decided not that she wouldn't go back, but that she wouldn't take her husband back. A shift in her mother's view of herself had occurred which Coral had witnessed, and this was enough for her to accept that the threat she had feared had gone. In this way the support given to a young person, which in some measure purports to eradicate fear by impressing the young person with a feeling of safety, is crucial.

FEARFULNESS AND BEHAVIOUR

Fears seem almost to evaporate at times, probably because a behaviour has been found which diminishes the feeling. Rachman (1998) explains that behaviour which successfully reduces fear will be reinforced and will be strengthened. Karl felt scared when he went to live in the refuge:

I started playing with the other children that was there...we used to do puppet shows.

Karl was able to 'ignore' his scared feelings as he played. He found that he could, and so he continued to play and spend time with the other children:

...there was this woman like that who came in every week and she done different things with us and I like painted a shirt and that with like fabric paints.

He had similar feelings when he knew his mother had decided to leave, and sensing his mother's fear, he too lived in dread of his father finding out. There was the time before, when his mother had 'got caught' when she had tried to leave. He reflected on the risks. Unlike the fear he had at the refuge which he could ignore, this other fear had remained for 'three or four years', supporting the idea that his previous experiences had prolonged and intensified his feelings of disquiet and inadequacy (McKeating 1970). Fearfulness becomes a festering influence, an irrational dread:

I'm still worried about him (dad) finding out where we live… Mum's got a new boyfriend…I mean husband now…that's good… (Karl)

FEARFULNESS AND CLOSE RELATIONSHIPS

Fear which is more forward-looking but which is rooted in painful experiences is spoken of with sadness. Relationships have been both damaging and lost. Fathers have had their place removed, but their influence remains:

That's why I don't call him dad anymore unless I'm with him. I don't believe he's my dad. I'm nothing like him. That's what I'm scared of now… I don't really want a girlfriend… I want one but I don't think I should have one 'cos I treat her like my dad did. (Terry)

If your dad was violent, you'll be violent when you're older. (Terry)

…I just thought that I didn't want to grow up and marry or anything…because all men are the same… (Coral)

The transference of fear from one situation to another, from one relationship to others, is indicative of the intensity of the original fearfulness. Where there has been what Rachman (1998) calls a history of threat, there remains a bias favouring that threat. This develops into a form of vulnerability or proneness which leads to a continuation of those fears, and a generalisation of the application of the threat. The original threat may have receded, but Terry and Coral acknowledge the price which they feel impelled to pay. However, even in these cases of generalised fear, the young people were able to recognise an end to their fears:

…but then, now that I've met — I know there's other people out there that can help and that they're not just there to ruin our life… (Coral)

…I don't trust men after everything and, but he (the support worker) sat down and basically said, he basically showed me it was ok to talk. (Rose)

Significant relationships acted as an antidote to the generalised fears felt by the young people. As their worst fears were dismissed and repudiated by caring people, they were able to feel the empowerment which comes from overcoming suffering. They were then able to recognise that the generalisations were irrational and could be discredited by an acceptance of much-needed help and support.

Scott accepted help because he recognised that he needed it. His anxiety and anger had become so overwhelming that he had been abusive to his mother and had been arrested. It was at this point that Scott's fearful anticipation of what might lie ahead motivated him to change:

>...I thought lots about it and um I decided I'm going to change now.

Rachman (1998) writes that fears do develop motivating properties. As Scott accepted help, he found that the support workers were 'very impressed' with him and he continued to successfully reduce the fear of prison and punishment, whilst increasing his own moral strength (ibid., p.57). In this way, Scott's fear energised his behaviour and he was able to stay motivated so that he was able to make what he had come to realise were necessary changes.

Factors that contribute to emotional instability associated with fearfulness can be clearly viewed in the lives of these young people. When faced with experiences which result in acute fears, young people will need reassurance, support in helping them to feel safe, and opportunities to reflect on how they might manage to overcome their fearfulness. On the one hand it will be necessary to reassure them that their feelings are right and justified, but on the other hand it will be essential to provoke and channel their thinking to enable them to participate in the development of their own wellbeing.

Aggressiveness

Bowlby wrote, 'All those who respond to a loss with...anger, a feeling of guilt for having been in some degree responsible, is playing a part' (1981, p.363). The association between fear and guilt has been drawn previously, but now there would appear to be a similar interdependence or link between anger and guilt. The emotionality of anger and fear may result in a complex interchange of feelings which may be difficult to untangle, decipher or differentiate. Aggressiveness may be the result of anger. However, 'Not all acts of aggression are preceded by anger' (Goldstein and Keller 1987, p.39). The motivation behind aggressiveness and aggressive acts and behaviour may be complex and varied, but it does seem that it may perhaps result from experiences of loss when the state of emotionality is dominated by anger, fear or guilt:

> *I threw a cup at my dad… And it just made things worse…so I stopped joining in with her (mum). (Coral)*

Aggressiveness may be seen as a form of behaviour which is directed toward the goal of harming or injuring another (Krahe 2001). Coral threw the cup at her dad, with the intent presumably of hitting him with it and hurting him. The occasion had been at a time when her dad was being violent to her mum. For the most part, Coral had been 'pushed away' during these episodes, but there had been times when she had directly witnessed the abuse, and on one occasion had stepped in to do what she could to stop the violence. She immediately observed the adverse consequences of her aggressive act, and never repeated it.

However, in a different situation, in a street somewhere in London, Coral again rebelled against her dad:

> *…I'd seen him, and we had a huge argument, a lot of crying and screaming in the middle of the street, so…*

The crying and screaming seemed to be describing her own feelings as she battled with her father. It was the last time that she had seen him, choosing to avoid contact with him since then. Her descriptions of her father reveal another feeling, a kind of frustration resulting from his several and continuous attempts to convince both her mother and her that he was going to change. However, the 'change' he achieved was short-lived:

> *He said he'd change before and this is the first time when we left…no…the second time and then mum took him back, and he changed like for two days and then he was back to his normal self. So I knew that it was all an act. He wasn't going to change.*

It is significant that this highly emotive experience in the street had been her last contact with her dad. It was her closing denunciation. Krahe (2001) describes this as a kind of aggression which is used to restore justice and also to end a state of frustration. For her, the crying and screaming were the culmination of years of emotional abuse and frustration brought about by her inability to intervene or change the situation. Her frustration would have been added to as her mother repeatedly gave her father more chances and a pattern of repeated failures and further abuse had occurred, culminating in an outpouring of aggressiveness which flowed when the opportunity arose.

The occasion of Coral's outburst has some interesting characteristics. Geen outlines how aggressiveness is the result of a need to retaliate following an attack from another person (1990, p.43). The retaliation may take the form of verbal aggressiveness or an insult or it may be physical. There may be haranguing or badgering. As Coral felt sufficiently empowered to retaliate, she was able to recognise the perfect moment. Her separation from her dad had been implemented by her mum. Her mum had put a stop to any contact. Coral had begun to build a life beyond the discord and stress of her past life. It appears that she was perfectly placed to 'turn tables' on her dad.

Geen (1990) goes on to describe how research on family violence has indicated that the family influences aggression in children in two ways. First, children are 'trained' in aggression. Family life provides situations which elicit aggression, and if aggressiveness is apparent in family life, children and young people are more likely to exhibit aggression. Second, where there is family violence, a stressful and aversive situation is created which may result in discord between all family members (Geen 1990, p.49).

ELICITORS OF AGGRESSION

Coral does in fact talk very little about feelings of aggressiveness, but it seems clear that in moments of deep frustration and strong inner desires to avenge, she is moved to hurt her dad. Geen explores the idea of elicitors of aggression which arise out of interpersonal conflict. Examples given are frustration, attack and harassment (1990, p.xii). The circumstances of Coral's battle with her dad appear to indicate the possibility of the presence of all of these elicitors. Her dad had searched her out at a time when she was staying with a relative close by:

> ...and he was like kind of hanging around in that area, and I'd gone to the shop and I'd seen him...

Her dad had been told that she was in the area, and had deliberately tried to see her without any planning or warning. The feelings which had been experienced by Coral when she'd 'seen him' must have been very powerful. She had not been prepared in any way for his appearance and she had been confronted by him. Earlier she had confided her longing for a loving relationship with her dad:

I was upset because I obviously love my dad but I knew that it (leaving him) was the right thing and that if she (mum) didn't do it then, she never would.

Her loyalty and love for her dad was stretched beyond her ability to feel it. Confusion and pain resulting from years of powerlessness, frustration and hurt had caused her to argue fiercely with her dad, and reject all possibility of any future happiness:

...when I was arguing with dad I just thought that I didn't want to grow up and marry or anything...because all men are the same...

This strongly negative emotional state created the potential for aggressiveness and it would seem that Coral's background of abuse motivated her reaction (Geen 1990). Ridgway writes of young people who sometimes react in this way. 'They've learnt in their families that the only way to communicate is to hurt others, because they have been hurt themselves' (1973, p.33). The aggressiveness is a way of protesting, and 'all their words are angry words' (ibid., p.67).

AGGRESSIVENESS AND RELATIONSHIPS

Scott confided that all his relationships at home and at school were problematic because of his 'not being nice':

Lately because I used to be...a pain in the... Because I wasn't really nice towards my family and school was really rubbish and I wasn't being nice towards my teachers... I was using abuse towards my mother. I wasn't really proud of that and I had to get arrested.

No one appears to have been immune to Scott's 'pain'. His words and his behaviour reflect the only way left to him to communicate with others and so he uses his suffering as a vocabulary. His words are angry words. His relationship, particularly with his mother, is stained by aggressive abuse. When asked how he felt at this time he could only string together a series of painful feelings.

The anger was there but it was splattered with sadness and anxiety which appeared to act as precursors. Aggressiveness for Scott was a way of communicating and possibly a safety valve too. Where there are high levels of emotional arousal, aggression can become a way of defusing feelings (Geen 1990, p.1).

Scott learns an alternative means of coping once he sees the consequences of aggressiveness:

*But lately my attitude has been changing, so…it's been good…and I thought a
lot about it… I decided I'm going to change now, because this is a bit silly and
lately I've been getting really well.*

Thinking for Scott was a crucial element in changing his aggressive coping
behaviour. He admitted that he still argued but 'just the odd occasional
teenage arguments' with his mum. The desire to hurt back had become
a desire to help and support other young people. How did this come
about? It seems likely that his focus at some point moved from inner
confusion and emotional turmoil to the emotional turmoil of others like
him. This needs to be accompanied by a level of maturity, and security,
which enables the young person to step outside themselves and become
aware of others' needs. Seemingly this was done through a persistent and
consistent availability of appropriate support which enabled the switch of
focus to take place.

AGGRESSIVENESS AND HARM

The dissipation of aggressiveness is also present in Rose's story. Aggressive
feelings can be directed towards oneself, and this seems likely as Rose
became intent on self-harm and injury. If we define aggressiveness as
the intent to harm, then it would appear that self-harm is intrinsically
aggressive. Motivations which incite self-injury are complex and varied,
and they are not clear. Rose expresses her reasons:

*I was going through a stage of self-harming…slitting my wrists and things like
that, but I don't…it wasn't properly or nothing. It was just to get attention back
then…*

Being 'a stage' indicates a transient or temporary part of Rose's story
which does, however, need to be recorded. Its significance and purpose,
which was 'to get attention', has to be an extraordinary revelation in
the light of her having to cope with her mum's depression and alcohol
misuse at the time, as well as the legacy of years of living with abuse. It
is probably impossible to imagine the intensity of Rose's feelings. Her
need for recognition, to be seen, to be nurtured was overwhelming, and
it is this need which must be met through a constant attention to the
vulnerability and strengths of the young person, and being willing to
value and appreciate their full identity.

Rentrew (1997) defines 'irritable aggression' as elicited by a variety of
stressors, for example pain, fatigue, frustration and deprivation; isolation

may produce and increase irritability. Rose's isolation at the age of 13 was almost complete. There had been only one friend with whom she could confide, and her mum was absent emotionally. Her aggressiveness had been turned upon her little sister, and her nastiness to her was a reflection of her loneliness and highly irritable state:

> I don't know why, I'd just get really angry with her really quickly and I'd just shout at her, and one time, I was really nasty to her, when we were left alone, I tipped Coke over her head and I...I think that's really nasty really...she was the closest thing I could have a go at, shout at and be really nasty to... I just had no other person really.

The isolation incurred from the circumstances of domestic abuse had been exacerbated by Rose's subsequent circumstances. Krahe writes, 'Children exposed to abuse and neglect were shown to display higher levels of aggression' (2001, p.54). The spiteful treatment of her sister Rose views as 'really nasty' and it occurred 'really quickly'. The irritable nature of what she did and the suddenness of what she felt indicates the presence of a number of stressors (Rentrew 1997) and an obvious isolation 'when we were left alone'.

The suffering of the past and the present had led to an emotionality which was both 'negative and antisocial that has little to do with mental health and well being' (Krahe 2001, p.10).

AGGRESSIVENESS AND VIOLENCE

The endorsement of beliefs which approve of aggressiveness (Krahe 2001, p.40) can be sensed as violence is defined by Terry. When asked about his sister's boyfriend's attitude to violence, Terry explains:

> Only if he wants to be (violent). He gets the choice. He's never violent to girls. He's violent to me but for a joke, he don't...

There are some kinds of violence which are not intrinsically aggressive, but Terry believes that some violence or aggressive behaviour is justified:

> If I was violent to anyone it would be to someone who was hurting someone for no reason.

Aggressive feelings and actions should be used to right wrongs. Terry has made a judgement here about the appropriateness of aggression under some circumstances. His emotionality is dependent upon his being able to distinguish the precise nature of aggression (Pugmire 1998) and how it should be realised. Pugmire gives an example of this when he writes, 'Hate can realise itself variously in elation, dejection, anxiousness or spite' (1998, p.12). How Terry shifts from one realisation of aggression to another is characteristic of his story. He believes that the safe expression of some of his feelings can be achieved through boxing and wrestling. This supports the idea of catharsis which proposes that any expression of aggressive feelings reduces the likelihood of subsequent aggression (Krahe 2001, p.213):

> ...my brother's in a mood or something, he tries to start a fight...I just push him over. I don't see the point of hitting him...what we're doing now is...it doesn't hurt us... It's keeping us out of trouble and we're playing but we're doing like boxing and wrestling... He loves wrestling, I love boxing... One rule is that he's not allowed to punch me...just get our energy away from fighting.

Using what appear to be aggressive experiences to divert energy away from actually fighting is a way of coping which works for Terry. As his anger is aroused, he adheres to the principle that 'attack is the best means of defence' (Bowlby 1981, p.363) and uses his feelings as an 'affective stress reaction' (Goldstein and Keller 1987, p.43).

Aggressive responses in the form of retaliation are another realisation of the emotion which Terry subscribes to. When his dad calls him a donkey, he calls his dad a donkey. When his dad publicly disowns his daughter, Terry publicly disowns his dad:

> That's why I don't call him dad anymore... I don't believe he's my dad.

Here are powerful images of Terry's wish to hurt back in response to hurt. However, it seems probable that Terry's various realisations of aggressiveness are learnt (Krahe 2001), but there is a deep fear of it also:

> That's what I'm scared about now... I don't really want a girlfriend... I want one but I don't think I should have one 'cos I treat her like my dad did. And it was on TV about the violence...if your dad was violent, you'll be violent too... but I've got his blood.

Terry was exposed to the most horrific violence and aggression perpetrated by his father against his mother. He too had suffered physical and emotional abuse. The abuse had continued during contact arrangements. He had learnt from his sister's boyfriend that there was another way, but the terrible fear remained that he would not be able to lose the biological and psychological heritage given him by his father.

So the conclusion appears to remain that for Terry a multiple connection to aggressiveness is his way of making sense of his life and his family. Although the realisations appear to possess conflicting ways of defining aggressiveness, Terry's story powerfully demonstrates the nascent and unique qualities exhibited as aggressiveness by individual young people.

Bitterness

Where abuse has been present, a child may find it difficult to distinguish and express appropriate emotions (Crompton 1998, p.144), resulting in interpersonal difficulties. When resentful feelings find expression in bitter words or violent action, the underlying motivations may vary or be unclear. However, there does appear to be a prevailing circumstance which Varma describes as a general sense of deprivation and loss which evokes 'hate, resentment and revenge' (1993, p.1):

> My dad gave all our stuff to this man across the road like our swings and that... and he said that my bike rusted away in the garage...but he sold, he gave our electric scooters away. He said that he was going to give it all to my auntie who lives in —. Then when my auntie went to meet him to get the stuff...um...he didn't have any...he wasn't even there.

BITTERNESS AND LOSS

Karl's bitterness at the loss of his possessions which clearly meant a considerable amount to him was attributable to the actions of his dad. The blame for the misfortune of his losses was being ascribed to his father without reservation. Accusations flowed and developed beyond the original wrongdoing. His dad had consolidated Karl's resentful feelings towards him by failing to care for his bike, which had rusted away, and then neglecting to keep to an arrangement which would have in some measure eased Karl's feelings of loss and abandonment. However, Karl's dad had become in his son's eyes an uncaring person who had blatantly and mercilessly increased Karl's feelings of loss:

I don't speak to him anymore...he only sent two letters that's all...he doesn't really care.

The humiliation of being let down in relation to loss is indicative of an understandable reaction to injury and indifference, which results in a complete breakdown of the relationship. Karl has withdrawn his good will towards his dad, and has decided on disapprobation and condemnation. Condemning his dad to silence, of not speaking to him anymore, is a form of revenge which suitably 'fits the crime' and which reflects Karl's bitterness. This selective form of inaction Varma (1993) asserts is a way of communicating dislike. This is also reflected in Karl's description of his dad before he left with his mum:

Because he never did anything. He would just lie down on the sofa and that was it... He was coming in from work on the sofa and that would be it, and whenever he wasn't on the sofa he was probably arguing with my mum or something.

Loss is probably a common denominator in relation to exposure to domestic violence. Losses occur within the full spectrum of human experience. Young people talk of the loss of their homes, their family members, their friends, their family pets, their schools, their teachers, their freedom, their privacy, their mothers, their sense of security, their possessions, their sense of belonging, their self-esteem, their confidence, their self-control, and the list continues. Losing anything which occurs beyond your ability to control, and which can be seen as a result of someone else's actions, inevitably leads to an overriding sense of resentment. They have the absolute right to object, and to be angry.

The task of those who are confronted by a young person's bitterness is to affirm it and to provide a way for the young person to express it and then help them replace the voids within them with something of value. This may take the form of rebuilding something that has been lost, or simply looking and finding worthy replacements. It may involve finding ways of remaining in touch with things that have not been totally lost, but which are just seemingly out of reach, but can be found with a little bit of effort. There are multiple solutions which can be looked for and discovered.

BITTERNESS AND RESENTMENT

Bitterness and resentment can be expressed in many ways. 'Teasing, mocking, deriding, jeering, ridiculing, sneering, taunting, belittling, blaming, accusing, criticising' (Varma 1993, p.73) are some of the behaviours which are used to communicate the underlying hurt and felt misfortune. Karl's feelings seem to be expressing criticism and sneering. He is overtly explaining and acknowledging his dissatisfaction with his dad, and his reasoning would in some measure logically justify his rejection of him. This justification and the seemingly honourable position taken up by Karl might perhaps act in some measure as a palliative, lessening the sorrow attending another loss, the loss of his dad.

Loss and injury do appear to be pivotal to feelings of resentment and bitterness. There may be a lessening of these feelings through an inner belief supporting the idea that the person responsible for the injury or loss is in some way abnormal. This can lessen the feelings of loss and bitterness:

> ...he (dad) was going to take her (mum) to the psycho hospital... You know the one near —. He tried to take her there...but I said he should be the one going there. (Terry)

Terry states how bitter he feels later as he describes how his dad lied about his daughter:

> He (dad) pretended he didn't know her (his daughter). I went 'You've got a daughter too', and he goes 'No I ain't.' That really hurt me. He used to always to do stuff like that...he pretended he didn't know her but thought it was a joke but it wasn't funny...it's not funny.

This last 'joke' by his dad was seen by Terry as a final injury which took away any vestige of remaining respect held by him for his dad:

> I didn't really have any respect for him anymore. I did have a little bit but I don't have respect for him anymore.

The final resolution of his feelings for his dad was controlled in part by Terry's acceptance of his father's need for some kind of psychological treatment. This was due to his recognition that his mother did not have a problem, but that his father did.

However, despite this realisation, which can allow the injured person to feel less resentment and malevolence towards the offender, Terry could not 'forgive or forswear the resentment' (Strawson 1974, p.6). He can only withdraw any goodwill he might have felt because of the overwhelming disapproval he felt for his warped and deranged parent.

Resentment can arise through feelings of unfairness and deprivation. Coral longed for a close relationship with her dad, but this longing was utterly frustrated:

> I would just listen to Eminem because he's so close to his daughter and he writes about her and sings about her and I used to just wish that dad would just be like that with me…but obviously he wasn't.

> He was a lot closer to my brothers than he was to me.

> When we was in the refuge we missed dad so mum started to try and get us to have contact with him… But then he would always like just get in the car with her and tell me to go into my auntie's house.

> …because when I was arguing with dad I just thought that I didn't want to grow up and marry or anything.

> I was upset (when mum decided to leave) because obviously I love my dad…

The desperate need for her dad's love and closeness to him remains a strangely powerful part of Coral's story. She appears to cling to the impossible as 'obviously' he couldn't be the dad she dreamed and hoped for. The loss and the emotional void and resentment which she clearly feels because of her father's inability to meet her need are devastating for her. Again, as with the other young people, she searches for some form of revenge and cuts physical ties with him. Physically and emotionally she tries to remove herself from his influence. She has withdrawn:

> Yeh, at the time he gave me his number and said that if I wanted to ring him or anything I could but at the time…because obviously when you see him, he's going to try and be all nice and it was making me think, maybe he has changed but then I got home and then I knew he hadn't really.

Coral chose not to contact her dad again, and she had had no contact with him since the terrible argument in the street at their last meeting. For her, the changing part was a prerequisite for a newfound closeness with him. This she had finally realised was not going to happen. Resignation had resulted, a reaction to her dad's indifference and inability to change and be close to her.

Injured and let down, Coral recognises the male oppression experienced by herself and her mother. However, her fear and resentment towards men had eased as she had met with men who 'were not just there to ruin your life'. Her life had been ruined for a time by her dad whom she loved. Her response to this terrible personal loss was to exclude him from her life (Varma 1993).

In a general sense, resentment coupled with bitterness is a result of prolonged exposure to offending behaviour and attitudes which in the end cannot be managed, and some sort of solution has to be found. Young people need the strength to find means of counteracting the damaging consequences of abuse and negative relationships. It seems that there is a strong element which remains for some time in relation to the desire to make things work, but this over time cannot be maintained, and then the search begins to find a way of accepting that things are not going to work, and the bitterness which is formed by repetitive disappointment can be allowed to gradually dissipate. Young people will need understanding in relation to the bitterness they feel.

BITTERNESS AND INJURY

Bitterness attending injury and loss associated with their fathers was felt by all the young people. Rose's hatred was overtly directed towards those who represented the Social Services:

> I hated them. I hated them. I thought you are not taking me away from my family, especially my mum.

The Social Services had become involved in Rose's family through concerns about 'me and my sister being left alone...in the home...' Varma (1993) states that children and young people are capable of communicating their feelings in a sophisticated, strategic and crafty way (p.73). Rose's opinion of the questions that were being asked her was one based on mistrust, resentment and fear. She was asked one particular question, she recounts, which required her to be 'crafty':

> ...the Social Services asked me...who do you love better out of your mum and dad? And obviously I love my mum because I hated my step-dad, but because I didn't want to be taken away, I said I loved them both the same.

The outcome of this interchange was that Rose stayed with her mum. Her mum stopped leaving her and her sister alone at home. Rose had reasoned that if she had shown she had a preference for her mum, then there was a greater likelihood of her being taken into care, as her mum had been neglectful. Once the Social Services had been told that step-dad was still very much part of the picture it appeared to Rose that they lost interest. Rose had accomplished the removal of persons she deeply resented. It is interesting to note that Rose always refers to these people by their department. Her bitter feelings have depersonalised them, so that they have become people without any real identity.

In this instance, Rose is clear in her own mind about the cause of her resentment. There is less clarity when her sister and her step-dad become the significant players:

> *When my mum was pregnant with her...and then he (step-dad) came round and he like would put on a show and he'd like pretend like to play with me and things like that, and then I thought, ah, he actually does care about me... But then as soon as my sister come along, it was like she was his own flesh and blood, I was pushed out.*

Rose expresses her bitter resentment and humiliation at the injury of her step-dad's pretence followed by his rejection. As Varma (1993) states, humiliations of the past may lead to a need for revenge. Blame was assigned for the most part to her little sister, as she was an easily acquired scapegoat. When she was asked why she had been 'nasty' to her sister, she was unsure about her feelings:

> *...maybe it was because she was the only person I could take something out on, because I was always stuck at home with her and because I was so young...*

> *So I don't know if that's the reason because maybe I was jealous, I don't know.*

> *She was the closest thing I could have a go at, shout at and be really nasty to... I had no other person really.*

The emotional complexity caused by Rose's vulnerability becomes clear. She feels bitterness towards her step-dad who had pushed her out. Equally, she had felt isolated and denied the love of another person – she had no other person except her little sister. She resented being 'stuck at home' with her, with the expectation that she should provide the care for her when she was 'so young'. The life of a young carer is all about the deprivation of her own needs. Rose's story reveals the pressures and torments of a young person who was forced to be the adult:

> *I was the adult... Obviously, I've still got that adult instinct in me, but I always will have because I've had it since the age of five.*

Rose had managed to retain her relationship with her mother, through her willingness to forgive. Although injured by her mother's actions, she was able to 'talk more and we just bond more'. Twinges of guilt and resentment remain, however, as Rose explains her desire for more independence and stronger emotional ties with her friends:

I've kind of pushed my mum out which makes me feel really bad sometimes.

Resentment and bitterness are the opposites of gratitude (Strawson 1974). Perhaps, Rose can only forgive so much as there has been so little to be grateful for.

Concluding the disempowering emotionality contained within the constructs of fearfulness, aggressiveness and bitterness, there needs to be a final acknowledgement of the complexity, ambiguity and interrelationships which exist between the chosen emotions. Fearfulness has been found to be associated with aggressiveness and bitterness, and other associations have been revealed. Other named emotions such as guilt, resentment, jealousy, confusion and anxiety have been found to be intertwined with fearfulness, aggression and bitterness, and their effects have merged and appeared in individual ways. The individual nature of each young person's emotional experience in relation to disempowering emotions is clear, and needs to be viewed in the context of the labyrinth-like journey locating the suffering voice.

A means of deciphering what I have defined as a suffering voice may be to remember that children and young people communicate their feelings in complex and sophisticated ways. Sensitivity is especially needed as young people share those experiences which have resulted in fear, aggression and resentment. These feelings are just and need to be affirmed but also assuaged. Encouragement to view them as part of the healing process may be one way of helping young people accept them and then dismiss them.

Humanising emotionality and abuse: locating the healing voice

Before negotiating the territories associated with more positive feelings, there is a need to pause for a moment to reflect on the possibility that within an emotional traversing of a story there is intrinsically contained a link between those suffering, difficult, dark and troublesome emotions and those which embrace healing. Grof and Grof write, 'The positive feelings often seem all the more significant and intense when contrasted with the difficult ones encountered previously' (1990, p.46).

The implication here is that there seems to exist a longitudinal relationship between the two, that humanising and empowering emotions follow the darker, more troublesome territories. Stories do possess longitudinal elements and it would seem that most people have to delve into and experience the darker areas of life 'before they reach a state of freedom' (ibid., p.46). Humanising emotionality is focused on three constructs, those of compassion, hopefulness and peacefulness.

Compassion

Berlant defines the emotion compassion as a 'humanising emotion' (2004, p.1). If an emotion is to become humane, it will need to demonstrate consideration for others. This must be the hallmark of such an emotion, and compassion does exhibit a social relation which incorporates a sufferer and an onlooker. Further to this, the onlooker is affected by the suffering of another, and is brought to an emotional state which appears to demand a response which may lead to action. Fox (1990) describes compassion as learning interdependence. It consists in the realisation that we are not unique, that compassion is a core constituent of our common humanity. The togetherness feelings arising from or possibly leading to compassionate yearnings are perhaps the most crucial aspect of experiences steeped in pain, injury or suffering:

> ...She (my friend) has problems with her dad but she can't talk to me about it in case it brings up about my dad. (Coral)

Her friend is concerned about the emotional impact of her experiences on Coral, and withholds these experiences, as she responds to the suffering of Coral. Awareness of suffering does seem to have had a marked effect upon the actions of the friend, but what is most interesting is the awareness of Coral as to why her friend should remain distant around the causes of Coral's suffering:

> *I say to her all the time that if she needs to talk she can but…I think she's worried.*

The friend is an instrument of compassion and anxiety, which counter one another and prevent the full expression of compassion which might involve both young people sharing and exchanging their common suffering. Fear overcomes one and interplays with compassion, allowing a revised, limited form of compassion to exist. Nevertheless, compassion is present, and exhibited by a caring concern for Coral.

COMPASSION AND EMPATHY

> *There was a time when a girl was all upset and I helped her out and after all she was mean to me and she said, 'Why are you so kind?' and I said because you're my friend. So she stopped being mean. (Scott)*

Compassion in its fullest sense appears to be unconditional. As Scott reached out to the suffering friend, he was met with a 'mean' response. But it in no way affected the stream of compassion which Scott felt:

> *I've helped out quite a lot of my friends. I persuaded my friend to stop self-harming their self.*

The act of persuasion had followed the feeling of compassion. Scott's feeling voice of compassion had led to powerful outcomes, which he saw as being very significant:

> *When I started to help my friends – I thought I'm pretty good at this… I was doing pretty well.*

Scott's story describes the tremendous outcomes for him and for his friends, due to the inner prompting of an emotion which led him from his own suffering to the suffering of others. Scott clearly expresses the pleasure which comes from relieving the pain of others. It is a remarkable outcome which at this stage can only be described in simplistic terms. However, there is evidence to support the more complex idea that the link between the suffering of one to the suffering of another is a prerequisite to being able to feel compassion, and that compassionate feelings can only exist where there have been personal experiences of suffering.

As interpretive insights are gained and developed, Scott's emotional journey from abused to abuser to compassionate friend will need to be individualistically constructed step by step. However, the stress at this point needs to be placed on the power of emotions to completely redirect lives:

> *I was really nasty to her (my sister)…but I'm trying to make up for it now… 'cos like I try to be there for her now. (Rose)*

Rose demonstrates guilt at one level because it would be logical to assume that her wish to make amends for being 'really nasty' was a direct result of feeling bad about her behaviour. However, guilt on its own is not necessarily a humanising emotion, and it therefore appears that Rose is feeling something other than or more than guilt. Her responsibility towards a younger sister, 'being there for her', signifies a move to feeling compassion towards someone less powerful than herself, who has suffered at the hands of all those close to her.

Her own identification with the suffering, her own knowledge of the pain of her sister, and the part that she accepts she has played in that suffering have all assisted her in being able to identify that she needed to make some sort of emotional and social recompense. She recognises and acknowledges the interconnectedness between herself and her sister. She had to be 'there' for her sister. This kind of understanding Fox terms 'a primary component of compassion' (1990, p.25).

The complex interplay between compassion and guilt is voiced by Rose in more than one way. Her story reveals a new-found independence which is bringing her new friends and good experiences, and which brought about an awareness of her identity in a new way:

> *I have been able to be myself…it was like I started going out with friends more and they were showing me different things.*

Her identity was becoming apparent to her through new relationships, 'becoming herself really', but this had come to her at the cost of 'pushing' her mum out:

> *I've kind of pushed my mum out, which makes me feel really bad sometimes but then I…feel like when my mum had all that time to have…to have all the time she wants with me but she never took it…she pushed me out…so I'm not trying to get back at her or nothing but I feel it's ok.*

Rose feels 'really bad', but this is softened by the knowledge that the past has in some measure given her permission to act in the way she has. The loneliness and sense of abandonment are measured against the joys of independence and friendship. The latter are weightier and provide a convincing confirmation of the rightness of her chosen course. With that confirmation, there can only remain a small vestige of guilt.

Rose is not seeking vengeance. There is only a trace of bitterness invoked by her mother not wanting to use the time once available to be with her daughter. She does, however, recognise that some might interpret her actions as being vengeful, and is conscious of the outward appearance of her life. Her compassion towards her mother is evidence of her recognition of the affinity and interdependence between them, that her happiness is somehow dependent upon her mother's:

> ...as long as I'm happy and as long as my mum's happy. I mean she's obviously going to have ups and downs in her life but then I'm going to be there to support her but as the child at the same time...

Rose has a plan which involves her being available to her mother, whom she discerns as in need of support sometimes. Despite her life becoming richer and happier in its own right, Rose incorporates past responsibilities and any associated suffering into her plan because she feels it is the right thing to do. The ethical nature of her view reveals a compassionate morality which cannot dismiss the pain of the past. Thomas Aquinas stated that compassion is not pure feeling, but it also implies moral decision-making followed by doing. Just as Rose weighed in the balance past suffering and present joys, she was able to recognise the importance of not entirely trying to forget the past, and of the need to continue to act upon it. This view of her emotional story seems to be derived from her relationships with her mother and her sister.

This interconnectedness is also reflected upon by Terry:

> My sister's boyfriend...he's been a lot of help 'cos he, he was in worse than me...and he taught me how to get through it.

The acceptance that someone who has had things worse than you can 'help' you expresses an awareness of the link created by suffering. As two abused individuals the connection is derived apparently from the abuse, and an acceptance of the other which in the case of Terry was far from his natural inclination:

'Cos he's coloured and I used to never have respect for coloured people. If I see them now, I get to know them.

Compassionate recognition of the worth of another based on shared experiences of abuse overrides a firmly held prejudice. The 'help' that was given was accepted and valued by Terry, and ultimately led to a significant change of view, based on an emotional turnaround from disrespect and suspicion to respect and admiration. The significance of this cannot be overestimated. Terry displays an interconnectedness with his sister's boyfriend which is powered by the ability to understand each other's suffering and which allows the one who has got through it to show compassion, and help the other. As a result, the relationship which seemingly had begun with a negative opposition to 'coloured people' has undergone a major shift to acceptance and appreciation. Terry was happy to be accepted by one whom he had previously disapproved of and had wanted to discount:

I said, could I be in his gang? …and he said, you can be in my gang (laughs quietly).

Empathy and compassion have revealed themselves as supportive companions in the lives of the young people. Their capacity to reach out to others and find a means of understanding the place where others stand is remarkable, and possibly needs to be viewed as a consequence of suffering. It is, I believe, a fact that suffering may assist in acquiring the ability to empathise with those who suffer. The negative effects of suffering already described form barriers to empathy. However, when young people are persuaded that their experience may be strengthening, and also provides them with abilities which others do not possess, then their own healing and the possibility of their involvement in the healing of others may begin.

COMPASSION, EMPATHY AND JUSTICE

Berlant (2004) states that compassion is linked to the rights of others. As experiences are inherently unstable and our day-to-day survival is characterised by social and economic insecurity, there is inequality all around us. Towards those who are less fortunate, there may be an awakening consciousness based upon an emotional response. Individuals are 'affected' by the suffering of another. Fox refers to this as 'compassionate justice' (1990, p.11), which is a desire to move towards equality guided by the assumption that all human beings are equally human, and therefore possess equal fundamental rights.

Recognising the rights of another was clearly demonstrated by Terry's sister's boyfriend, and Terry, having received the teaching of how to get through it (past suffering), was moved to reciprocate. As individuals identify with the rights of others, and perceive inequalities, discrepancies and violations, they may react in compassionate ways and possibly feel pleasure and relief from unwanted, unpleasant feelings as assistance is given and recompense made.

This aspect of compassion may also be discerned when Coral talks about what happened when she spoke to her mother about leaving her father:

> I think she knew all along that we had to get away, but I think she was staying there for our sake.

Her mother had decided to stay because the needs of the children had been more important than her own. Coral had seen a loving mother sacrifice her own life for her children, and had supported her in that decision for a while. However, the pain she had felt at witnessing the domestic violence against her mother proved too much for her:

> Well I was the one actually who told my mum that we had to get away and tried to make her do it.

The rightness of the decision to leave was unequivocal. Nothing could stand in the way of putting this decision into action. In this way, 'making' her mum do it was fuelled by a passionate reaction which was drawn from both witnessing her mother's misery and a firm knowledge that it was right. The moral outrage of what was happening had resulted from Coral's compassionate desire to end her mother's suffering. She did what she had to do:

> ...when she realised that I'd said it (that we had to get away) I think it just made it clear that she had to get clear away.

The 'clear'ness of this statement seems to demonstrate the single-mindedness of Coral at this time. The clarity of the rightness of the decision coupled with the clarity of her own moral position evoked by compassion resulted in a clear pathway ahead, to get away.

The compassion Coral felt for her mother changed their lives. Coral had entered into the suffering of her mother, she had identified with it, she knew it and she shared it. A oneness existed of deep feeling and ultimately of celebration. When she was asked how she felt when her mother believed what she was saying, she laughed:

Happy…that we were finally going to get away.

Joy and happiness which come from celebratory experiences can be experienced by those who have relieved the pain of others. Asked if he would change his past life if he could, Scott describes a present which celebrates the past:

I don't know… I might change something but if I change I might not be able to help people with what I want to do.

His desire to help people is a product of his own suffering and he recognises that the former would be put into jeopardy if the latter had not occurred. The link appears to be the formation of a lasting compassion which finds expression in his present life as he focuses on alleviating others' suffering. His life is all about 'doing' what he has learnt, and applying what has removed his pain to those who are suffering now. This ongoing compassion should be viewed as a celebration of a life once tormented but which is now rescued and productive.

An identification, an empathic connection to the suffering of another, appears to be present in the voice of Scott. It also seems to be characteristic of Coral's response to her mother, and Rose's view of her mother and sister. The sister's boyfriend also reacts to Terry in a way which indicates a close identification with him. Nussbaum (1996) asserts that this identification allows the viewer 'to judge what others need in order to flourish' (cited by Boler 1999, p.160).

Terry explains the way his sister's boyfriend helped him:

And he's been talking to us every time we were upset…and tells us what it's like when it's better…he says everything is gone. All the stress is gone…so he makes us look forward to that and then we are not upset, simple words.

Terry recognised that he was helped in a way that was simple, but very effective. He was not upset anymore. Being able to judge what is needed is an invaluable gift which Terry was able to describe. He recognised what had been done for him to 'flourish', and was grateful. In his book *Death and Loss*, Leaman (1995) describes how from the point of view of the young people interviewed, few had found any teachers particularly helpful at the time of their loss. One example, Julie, had wanted to grieve quietly, and did speak of one particular teacher who had expressed her sympathy through ordinary actions. Julie had found this teacher especially helpful. Probably the essence of knowing what others need in order to flourish lies in recognising the individual, and the differences that may exist as well as those commonalities which result in identification.

Every young person will respond to abuse and suffering in their own particular way. Perhaps the issue of knowing how to respond rests in the compassionate blending of a personal empathic identification with the individual with a respectful recognition of the uniqueness of each individual.

It appears that forms of personal identification require the emotion of empathy, an ability to imagine and associate with the feelings of another. Connections can occur within relationships which demand no action. However, compassion seems to involve empathy as a prerequisite to a motivating power to act. It seems to be true that the connectedness created by an empathic identification with another resolves itself in some way to become a force which enables an individual to feel in such a way as to be compelled to action.

The force seems to be created by a moral position which impels the righting of a wrong. The action is driven by a powerful impulse, a passionate realisation that the miseries of others are in some way connected to our own and that we bear some responsibility. However, this transition from empathy to compassion does not always automatically occur. Karl refers to his father's behaviour as interfering with this process:

> *We don't get on well (my sister and I)…because of my dad…um…affected the way we was with each other in — and my dad was like always on the sofa and that…*

Karl's repetition of his father's behaviour as always being on the sofa, which he mentions three times, reflects a preoccupation with something which had destructive repercussions but which clearly had a powerful impact on him. Whether this impact was a result of pity or some form of empathy is unclear, but Karl did continue to see his father and talk to him on the phone after the family break-up. His awareness of his father's disinterest grew piece by piece as Karl builds an image beyond 'the sofa', which reveals an erosion of any positive feelings he might have had:

> *I don't speak to him anymore…he only ever sent two letters that's all…he doesn't really care…*

My dad gave all our stuff to this man across the road, like our swings and that...

My dad said we had to give it (the dog) away.

Karl's observation of his dad prior to this erosion embodies a view of him which seems to physically place him close to his father's behaviour. There is evidently a feeling of connectedness to his dad, which might be construed as empathy. There is a strong feeling that Karl had at some point almost put himself on the sofa with his dad. There is, however, no sign of compassion. What is it that prevents the growth of empathy or sympathy into a passion which would fortify and strengthen the connection and lead to a desire to relieve his dad's pain? The answer lies in what is required to answer the need for justice. As empathy is acted upon by those values which determine what a person sees as right or wrong, there may be a switch from a position of aligning themselves with a person to a position of repudiation. How could Karl remain on the sofa with his dad, when he could see the effects of that position on his family and himself? The compassion had taken him to his father's side, had led to a form of empathy, but had ended with a rejection of those things which had brought suffering into his life, and an acknowledgement that in order for consequences to be logical and deserved, compassionate feelings have to be subordinated to the need for justice.

As we watch the confusion caused by suffering, there is a need to reflect on how young people come to the decisions they make. Their sense of what is right and fair is keen, and this may be the motivating force which underpins their actions.

COMPASSION AND PITY

Another possibility which may thwart the generous growth of empathy born of compassion lies in an emotion which has some confusing elements. Pity is an emotion that would naturally get in the way of compassion. Pity has been defined as lacking the oneness of deep feeling, mind and action which are present within compassion. Pity seems to exhibit a desire for separateness.

Karl saw his dad as suffering, but weak and inferior also. A close association or connection with him would bring no reward, and would seemingly bring suffering upon himself. Removing self or moving away from an object of pity can be seen as a form of self-preservation but it does reveal an underlying lack of concern or interest in the sufferer. Fox refers to pity as a form of condescension, a 'disguised gloating' (1990, p.2). This seems a harsh definition, but when compassion is absent it seems likely that suffering is viewed as a state of inferiority and impoverishment and it should be shunned.

There would appear to be a separation of the individual from the suffering. The suffering is seen in isolation. Berlant talks of 'scenes of vulnerability (which) produce a desire to withhold compassionate attachment, to be irritated by the source of suffering in some way' (2004, p.9). Attachment is withheld, and suffering is viewed dispassionately. Karl clearly saw the suffering of his father, but was not constrained to alleviate it. He withdrew emotionally, and later was able to outwardly remove all emotional ties to his father and voice only disparaging views of him. If it was pity that Karl felt, it was only a few steps away from the emotions of irritation, anger and ultimately indifference.

Compassion, on the other hand, is resilient, immovable and self-sustaining. At this point, the question arises which asks, why is it that pity appears to replace compassion in certain circumstances? The ethical component of compassion seems to be at the heart of this question. The connections that are made between the vision of what is seen as 'the overall good' and a personal commitment to respond seem to be a critical feature of compassionate feeling. Making decisions about how to respond to suffering depends upon a personal view creatively and imaginatively constructed. Robinson (2008) writes that this view is based upon intrinsic beliefs and community relationships. These links he feels have received little attention from researchers:

> ...there has been little attempt to relate virtues systematically to the affective domain (for example, through an analysis of empathy) and still less to see how they relate to belief systems. (Robinson 2008, p.9)

Emotions which emerge from what is seen as good or virtuous, which in turn are in some way connected to beliefs, will be discussed fully at the conclusion of this chapter.

COMPASSION AND HAPPINESS

There is a strong link between compassionate feelings accompanied by action and happy, sometimes joyous, feelings voiced by the young people. Coral described how she had 'told' her mum that she should get away from her dad, because she could not bear to see her mum suffer anymore. When it became clear that her mum was going to follow Coral's direction, Coral laughed out loud at the memory of that moment:

> *Happy (small laugh) that we were finally going to get away.*

Terry showed a more direct emotionally happy outcome at the time of the abuse towards his mother:

> *She used to call me her favourite...her magic boy, because when she was sad I knew exactly what to do...just smile and give her a hug and anything like that.*

His ability to exhibit a happy, cheerful response to his mother's sadness was an isolated example of Terry's ability to feel pleasurable emotions which were expressed only once in his story. He illustrates his compassionate yearnings for his mother's safety and wellbeing consistently and constantly. Only once does he remember these experiences in terms other than painful.

As he recollected his ability to smile and be a 'magic boy' in direct response to his mother's pain, he demonstrated that compassion can neutralise suffering, or at least act as a buffer. It can overcome sorrow and the effects of pain in some measure. Affection and a positive display of cheerfulness can be unlocked from an inherently painful experience. An image is drawn of mother and son happily hugging and smiling together despite the pain of recent events.

Robinson (2008) describes how suffering can be transcended. His feeling is that there needs to be a conceptualisation of how life ought to be, together with an understanding of what constitutes the suffering:

> The suffering of another enables us to be open to the real presence of the other and leads to the development of responsibility for the other. However...suffering is an inevitable and profound part of our lives and...compassion and empathy are the only way of making sense of it. (Robinson 2008, p.182)

Terry cannot help but want to take care of his mother:

> *I just depend on making sure she's safe.*

> *I used to push him (dad) away and everything, but if I didn't do it and my mum really would get hurt... I used to cry 'cos I thought I could have stopped that but I didn't.*

That's why I was scared about her (mum) meeting another man 'cos I don't want to see her like that again.

Terry's expressions of his feelings in relation to his sense of responsibility for his mother are deeply moving. His feeling voice is full of anguish and regret. However, there is also a clear message that he felt his efforts were not in vain. He was continuing to feel just the same, making sure his mum is safe, despite being told by his support worker that 'I shouldn't do that but I like doing it.'

Making sense of the pain around his mum and himself seems to demand a continuation of his compassionate overseeing of their situation even though the perpetrator is no longer in direct contact with his mother. In time it is probable that the need for this interdependency will decrease as the suffering becomes more distant and its memory becomes diffused. Terry's sense of responsibility will diminish in relation to his mother's suffering, but his capacity for compassionate responses will probably remain.

Young people need happy experiences, in order for them to have the kind of balance in their lives which would lead to an overall sense of wellbeing. This can be achieved through regular ongoing instances of things that cheer – young people need to have fun with people who care, with compassion and joy intermingled as they enjoy being close to people.

COMPASSION RECEIVED

Compassion is given and received. The young people's emotional response to compassion received is complex and seems to be dependent upon the evolving relationship between them and the giver. Those relationships which embraced the idea of support and care, particularly involving professionals such as teachers or workers for voluntary organisations, were described in very positive ways. There is a very strong element of appreciation and recognition of the part these workers played in solving problems and initiating changes which proved to be positive:

I have had — to myself…she is someone I can trust really well. I've been seeing her for about…four years now. It was really good. (Scott)

I think most of the support came from — and I think that really helped me because I was keeping a lot of stuff inside…and now that it's all out and I've told — everything…I can kind of move on. (Coral)

I know there's other people out there that can help... (Coral)

At first I felt really worried but then there was... like really nice people there (in the refuge). (Karl)

Think like he's (support worker) helped me a lot... better. (Karl)

I've got a lot more confident because he said to me you shouldn't let anyone put you down and... it has worked. (Rose)

The adults who were able to alter the young people's lives in such radical ways demonstrated a willingness to listen and build trust. The help which was felt was reliable and could alleviate anxiety. It was also able to build confidence through sensitive encouragement and advice. Being 'nice' probably refers to an adult who demonstrates reliability and genuineness. Young people have an incisive perception and are probably able to discern any form of deception.

The value that is given to particular adult workers is high and humbly recognised. With the acceptance of the help given, the young people acknowledged that they were indeed in need of help. Each of the young people expressed different needs. These included a cry for help through self-harming, a need to manage his anger better, a need to get horrible experiences out into the open, a need to stand up for himself, a need to be a teenager and a need to become more independent and confident. Solutions to meeting these needs were offered and some accepted. What follows is dramatic and heart-warming.

The young people clearly state that as recipients of compassionate interventions by caring professionals, they have had some of their critical needs met, their suffering has been lessened and their lives have become happier.

Hopefulness

Suffering from abuse has been likened to torture. Analyses of the perpetration and resultant effects of abuse have drawn attention to the many similarities between victims of domestic abuse and torture victims. Torturers are inherently intent on eradicating every vestige of hope. Their game is to undermine through degradation, isolation, threats, displays of total power and the infliction of pain. Their ultimate purpose is to bring about despair, a belief that all is lost and that the only way out is to give in and surrender to the demands of the torturer. The victim possesses a sense of personal resignation with an abandoning of self-worth and identity which leads to their psychological, emotional and mental bondage. The point is reached when the victim becomes a nonentity with an absolute loss of autonomy and personal agency. All control and power is now held by the perpetrator.

The disempowered victim would appear to be in a hopeless situation. Victims of domestic abuse are undermined just as victims of torture, through degradation, isolation, threats, never-ending anxiety and displays of total power. Survivors talk of these experiences:

I had lots of worries.

Not very happy...worried, miserable...angry.

I usually got shouted at or I got threatened.

I had to see my mum getting hurt or something.

Horrible (home).

Because I hated seeing her and hearing it (domestic violence).

She (mum) would always reassure me that it wasn't my fault but...I did still feel guilty.

I was scared that he might come back.

We had a huge argument (dad and me), a lot of crying and screaming in the middle of the street.

My mum was being sick every time she went to the toilet.

Crying nearly...every single second of the day.

It's about talking down to them...my dad wanted to control me.

I've always had abuse.

I used to cry 'cos I thought I could have stopped that but I didn't.

He said it was my fault that he was beating up my mum.

Clearly, there is more than enough to dispel any vestiges of hope, one would suppose, and yet this is far from the reality of stories shared with me. I would be inclined to believe that there is a generality pertaining to feelings of hope amongst young people who have been exposed to domestic violence, as my overall experience renders this very likely.

HOPEFULNESS, AFFLICTION AND PAIN

The grimness of the young people's lives is indisputable. Peltomaki (2008) speaks of this kind of suffering as something much worse, as affliction. The definition which is used to describe 'affliction' is pain which scars all dimensions of a person's life. Affliction is an extreme condition which leaves its victims powerless and with no escape. It is stated that 'Affliction permeates the soul and affects one's future direction, one's destiny and one's hope' (ibid., p.223). It is extraordinary that hope can be silenced but hopefulness does, however, remain in the voices of the young people. It is what Peltomaki (2008) describes as a 'clinging' hope. There is a feeling that there may be someone who might understand the pain or at least see the suffering, and possibly work to bring an end to it:

> *When I was young, I used to think to myself this isn't going to be for ever 'cos as soon as I'm old enough I can leave and I always looked at that picture when I was little and the person that gave me that idea was my auntie. (Rose)*

Rose's auntie saw the pain and was able to ignite the 'clinging' hope into a picture which embodied hopefulness. The pain would end and Rose had it within her power to end it. Rose describes how she always kept the 'picture' in her mind which had been given to her by her auntie. Hopefulness had become a tangible thing, a lingering image which embodied her escape and her freedom from pain. Her affliction had not entirely prevented her from believing in the future and she was able to accept the truth of the 'picture'.

This vision which Rose held on to had the power to sustain her. As dreams do, so the 'picture' took her somewhere else beyond the present reality to a place where there were untold possibilities:

> *You can do whatever you want and I've always looked at that picture.*

It is remarkable that the young people demonstrate hopefulness in the face of torturous experiences which are inflicted upon them by those who should be caring for them. The loss of this care and the security of family relationships associated with it appear to create an emptiness and a silence which results from the isolation caused by unspeakable events.

Coral describes her life as being friendless with no opportunity to talk about her experiences until long after separation from the perpetrator. When she was asked if there was anyone that she could speak to other than her mum, she replied:

> *Nobody else, nobody else at all.*

I didn't think I needed to speak to anyone else.

I was keeping a lot of stuff inside and didn't really want to talk to anyone about it.

I didn't really have a friend that I could talk to or anything...

As a forced isolation takes hold of the young person's ability to communicate with others, Coral holds firmly to a hopefulness which surrounds her mother. It feels as if there is a connection between an implicit trust which Coral holds for her mum and a thread of hopefulness:

I knew that it was the right thing (leaving dad) and that if she didn't do it then she never would... I knew this had to be the last time.

The trust in her mum's decision is almost complete, although she is still aware of her own and her mother's vulnerability:

I didn't want to talk about it because I was scared I would make her upset and I was scared that it might make her want to take him back again.

Despite the isolation and her fear and vulnerability, Coral remained open to experiences and people who would challenge her built-up perceptions of her life:

He made me see things differently... I didn't want to grow up and marry or anything because all men are the same, but then, now I've met — I know there's other people out there that can help and they're not there to ruin our life...

Her hopeful vision had allowed the penetration and acceptance of new experiences which might have been discounted and rejected if they had been based solely upon what was seen as a totally bleak and uncompromising past. Hopefulness is sometimes likened to a penetration of light in otherwise dark circumstances. The darkness and bleakness of life experiences which are predominantly characterised by affliction and suffering can be infused by the light of hopefulness. Israel (1995) describes this process as a relief from vile experience:

> Hope is like the first rays of sunshine breaking through the darkness of a lengthy night and lighting up the previously hidden landscape to reveal its naked beauty. (Israel 1995, p.55)

HOPEFULNESS AND LIGHT

The hidden landscape is hopefulness which is a view of what is being lived that magnifies the wonders of that life and also directs the gaze away from those things which cause despair and despondency. The view may be just a 'spark' but it is enough, Israel (1995) affirms, to dispel the darkness.

Terry describes the process of light coming into his life. His sister's boyfriend would talk to him and his younger brother:

> *And he's been talking to us every time we was upset or he's there and he takes us to a different room or something and sits down and talks to us. And tells us what it's like when it's better, and that's what we are looking forward to. He says everything is gone...all the stress is gone...so he makes us look forward to that and then we are not upset.*

Hopefulness exists beyond the present in 'a different room'. It's there that an important truth for Terry is shared and accepted. The truth of 'when it's better' is a fundamental element of his hopefulness. This element of anticipation within hopefulness is examined by Israel (1995). Hope he describes as a primary emotion, which combines desire and expectation. He writes that hope remains the most intimate of inner feelings. It has been described in the most eloquent terms which are immediately persuasive and expressive:

> Hope springs eternal in the human breast. (Pope, *An Essay on Man*)

> That invisible fecundity, that spring of living water that makes humanity capable of flowering, is hope. (Jessey 1978, p.9)

Obedience to this hope, of not 'if it's better' but instead 'when it's better', enables the person 'to live to survive, to endure and to stand up to life' (Peltomaki 2008, p.231).

Despair has not been allowed to overcome Terry completely. Instead, he and his brother are able to look forward to a brighter future, free of 'everything' in the past which has upset them and afflicted them. Robinson describes this aspect of hopefulness as 'empowerment for change' (2008, p.144), and it is clear that Terry sees what has happened as a change from a state of being upset in the present to being made to look forward to an end of suffering. The empowerment is given through an empathic recognition of the needed remedy. This is given as Terry is told what it's like when things are better. The result is changes in the present, a change in attitude, a change in his thinking and a change in his emotional state. Not only can Terry see the future as being better than the past, but the present is also better. Robinson writes, 'The primal ground of hope lies not in the future but in the present and above all in an other' (2008, p.144).

The making of the present hopeful is a task which should be an aim of all those who work with any young people. Instilling light when all around appears dark and grey is a process which needs to happen in the now, and can be achieved in individual and varied ways. Encouragement, praise, opportunities to develop talents, opportunities to be with other young people who have had similar experiences, and much more, need to take place. It is our duty to reflect on the needs of the young people we know, and through our closely interacting with them, we will be able to establish how to bring light into their lives.

HOPEFULNESS AND SPIRITUALITY

Swinton (2001) defines this form of emotionality in terms of spirituality; that spirituality is the process and development of an appreciation and awareness of the other, including the self.

Terry clearly identifies the author of the remedy as being the creator of the changes which take place. Terry's sister's boyfriend was able to 'model' the changes for Terry and his brother, and inspire hopeful feelings. He had his own knowledge of affliction and suffering and had obtained his own hopeful outlook and expectations. He could offer Terry a view of recovery and self-worth which would encourage him and help him to overcome his fear.

Karl's description of the family's escape to a refuge appears at first to be a matter-of-fact record of what happened:

> ...*someone in my family helped find a refuge, and there was one in — and one somewhere else but we like never knew anything about — so we thought it would be nice to come to —.*

Karl is clearly expressing a hopefulness around the choice of where they would ultimately live, and exhibits an evident faith in the outcome of the choice. Robinson writes that this form of hope is future orientated (2008, p.144). Karl uses the pronoun 'we' to determine how the whole family felt when the decision was made. The hopefulness felt towards the future appears to be dependent upon the strength of critical family relationships. 'We' in this instance indicates Karl's implicit trust and faith in his family's decision as well as a willingness to embrace the outcome despite being 'a bit scared'. A hopefulness ascribed to the future is not merely a blind optimism (Robinson 2008, p.144), nor is it a mindless vision of the future seen through rose-coloured spectacles (Mananzan *et al.* 1996). Degenaar writes that the forward thinking and feeling which constitutes hopefulness may be seen as 'a creative expectation' (1991, p.4).

Robinson (2008) discusses this creative or imaginative element of hopefulness, describing the ensuing consequence as possessing multiple pathways. A range of possibilities may be envisaged and considered. Through collaboration with others and by working through various possibilities, 'a feeling that things can be done' (ibid., p.146) emerges, and this can further fuel hopefulness. As Karl was hopeful at the time the choice of his future home was made, he remained constant to the idea that despite fears and worries, the pathway taken would be the right choice and lead to further pathways and choices, and 'things' could and would be done:

We came down to the refuge and then moved in there for seven and a half months…and then we got a temporary house just down the road from where I live now…and then…got another one like permanent, where we are now.

I've still got one friend who lives in — and he was from the refuge…

My mum's got a new boyfriend…I mean husband now…that's good…so we go places and that…we went to a Greek restaurant on…last week.

Karl announces the choices and pathways which have been 'good', and despite the huge feelings of loss which he undoubtedly felt, was able to imagine a future realistically drawn and hopefully expected. Karl concluded with his view of his family:

I think like it's improved a lot.

Karl's family had changed, through the changes that had been instigated by the family's choices. These changes within the family were evidence of the rightness of the pathways chosen. There remained within Karl remnants or vestiges of hopefulness, or perhaps hopefulness has regenerated itself into stronger and more resilient hopefulness.

Ackermann writes, 'Our actions again reinforce our ability to hope' (1996, p.144).

HOPEFULNESS AND WAITING

The expectancy which is part of the future orientation of hopefulness requires additional emotional expenditure. Waiting is companion to expectancy. 'Hope is also learning to wait' (Ackermann 1996, p.144). Waiting requires patience and endurance. It is an interesting phenomenon that the young people often refer to specific times. It appears to be a human characteristic that waiting may result in a propensity to clock-watch. How long we have to wait is a fact that our minds seem to want to consider and record:

> We came down to the refuge and then moved in there for seven and a half months. (Karl)

> Then we was living in a caravan park for two months. (Rose)

> We was put in a temporary house for I think it was six months. (Rose)

> He (dad) changed like for two days and then he was back to his normal self. (Coral)

> It was nearly two years ago and he (dad) haven't given it (divorce) to her (mum). (Terry)

As the young people patiently endured the wretched circumstances of their lives there is no doubt that their challenges were tightly associated with the necessity of banishing those things which sought to deprive them of hope (Ackermann 1996).

Coral is haunted by the possibility of her mother's return to her father. Terry is terrified that his mother might become involved with another abusive partner. Those things which seem to be designed to attack hopefulness remain and create oppositional forces which have to be 'wrestled' with (Ackermann 1996).

Again, the confusion young people feel about how to feel is prevalent. There will always be an opposition to feeling hopeful, but it is reasonable to suppose that through the efforts of the young person and those who want to strengthen them, the light need not be extinguished. Despair is a prerequisite for depression possibly, and so it remains critical that the young person is not left to fight the emotional battle alone.

HOPEFULNESS AND JUSTICE

The wrestle which is displayed by the young people can be seen by them firmly and fiercely holding on to and believing in justice. The relationship between hopefulness and justice is complex and requires some thought. In the context of suffering, 'restitutive' justice would appear to be relevant, as the young people and their mothers have suffered great losses and pain:

> She's (mum) changed 'cos she's split up with him (dad). She thought...he just wanted to control me, and I was like...'Well done'. (Terry)

> My dad wanted to control me. I wouldn't give it to him 'cos he's not winning. And he's realised now that if he talks down to me, I'll talk down to him. (Terry)

Terry is describing feelings which are based upon what he sees as wrongs being put right, justice in action. Whereas before, his dad caused immeasurable suffering, his mum has now recognised what is required to bring about a kind of restitution. It feels to Terry that there is a form of recompense in his mum's deeper understanding of her husband's abuse of her. This, coupled with her freedom and independence of him, formed a 'restitutive' justice. Similarly, he had carved out for himself a kind of satisfaction in being able to stand up to the father who had abused him daily. It would not be illogical to say that these actions were born of a desire to create justice, which would have been possible only with the possession of hopefulness which sustains and empowers.

Hopefulness can be seen to aid self-determination and allow transformation (King 1996). Terry clearly expresses a new identity and a new freedom. Wrestling against injustice and those feelings which seem to naturally attend it, such as despair and despondency, is one form of struggle which is fuelled by hopefulness. The struggles against apathy and shame can only be fought in the present which has not been allowed to become totally darkened:

> She said to me, she said go on, you can go into care, it was like she didn't care what happened to me...and my mum said I can't be dealing with you... I didn't really know what to do. I had a five-year-old little sister as well. (Rose)

Rose's struggle to remain fixed in her love for her mum despite apparent total rejection results in her subsequent actions to ensure her family stay together. Her mum remains the central figure:

I hated them (Social Services). I hated them. I thought, you're not taking me away from my family, specially my mum.

Rose lied to the Social Services because she believed it would allow her to stay with her mother. Her hope somehow lay in overcoming the shame and hurt she felt by enabling her family to be together, highlighting the critical importance of her mum and she being able to mend their relationship.

Rose describes the situation a little later on as unchanged emotionally. Her relationship with her mum does not appear to have become closer; there is no evidence to support the mending of their bond:

It was really depressing because mum was so depressed. She just felt really alone and...she just wanted to drink all the time... I was going through a stage of self-harming.

Her mum's aloneness even when her daughters were with her indicates a disinterest in her children which mirrored her earlier emotional abandonment of them. A lack of concern and an apathetic desensitization to the needs of her children were the result of the years of abuse.

Despite her mother's apparent indifference, Rose struggled against despondency and accepted help when it came her way. Her view was that she had 'found' herself, that she was able to be herself because she had been told, 'It's ok to be myself, it's ok to be a teenager.' She had been convinced and had readily embraced her identity as it had been revealed to her. Her hopefulness had lain in knowing that she was ok. The simplicity of the message belies its power. The message was received by Rose's struggling identity, a spark of hope which remained was ignited and she gained a new-found hopefulness:

I feel it's ok for me to do my own thing now and my mum hasn't got to be there all the time.

Rose's story supports Ackermann when she writes, 'Somewhere in the deepest recesses of the human spirit there lurks the gift, the power of hope, in the face of the most wretched circumstances' (1996, p.143).

Hopefulness has been linked to life itself. 'To lose hope is to lose life' (Ackermann 1996, p.144). The empowerment and autonomy which comes through hopefulness can be seen in the stories of the young people. Each one had been disempowered and nullified by violence. 'The taproot of violence is surely silence, of being vetoed and nullified and cancelled so that we have no say in the future of the community or of our own lives' (Brueggemann 2000, p.7). However, their stories capture the changes which represent the influence of hope.

Hope sees the suffering but it believes in the future (Peltomaki 2008). 'Obeying hope' allows the possibility of survival (ibid., p.231):

> *I want to talk about it (the abuse) and hopefully let it help other people... I feel it's always going to be there but I can kind of move on...and try and put it in the past. (Coral)*

Peacefulness

The word 'shalom' is a Jewish greeting or farewell, of welcoming and leaving peace behind. It encompasses wellbeing, human flourishing and fulfilment (Dorr 1990). Robinson (2008) defines it as possessing a sense of wholeness alongside a sense of justice. Fox (1991) describes the fusion of peace and justice as the creative capacity of compassion. The isolation of the emotion of peacefulness appears to be inherently problematic, as there appears to be a tendency to describe it in terms of its relationship with other emotions. The relationships are explained in such a way as to rely on peacefulness as being a constituent of another more 'basic' emotion, or as being recognised only when it is joined with another. Its effects therefore would seem to be complex and entangled, and feelings associated with it difficult to isolate and define.

However, in the stories of the young people, it seems evident on nearly every page. The evidence of a kind of calmness and tranquillity in the face of disturbing, often violent, experiences is clearly seen as the young people react in forgiving, often reconciliatory ways:

> *There was a time when my friend was being nasty to me and I helped him out. And there was a time when a girl was all upset and I helped her out and after all she was mean to me and she said, 'Why are you being so kind?' and I said because you're my friend. So she stopped being mean. (Scott)*

Scott sees the situation not in terms of retribution, where justice might have been better served if he had sought vengeful, equally mean responses to those young people who were being 'mean' to him. Instead he reacted in a creative way, transforming the emotional dynamics of the relationships, and causing the meanness to stop. The peacemaker, the pacifist, is revealed as Scott determines future events through the emergence of his forgiving acceptance of the situation. He restores a sense of peace to his circumstances and adds, 'So that was really good.' The goodness of what he sees he has done is indicative of an ethical stand which he has made which has found expression in his actions which are based on a determination to relieve suffering. His protest was a pacifist one. He resisted the impulse to seek revenge; he struggled against what many would see as an understandable reaction and sought harmony.

As the idea of inner peace is explored, it is necessary to recognise the wrapping together of peacefulness and other emotions. This is highly significant, and the calm, good feelings which are associated with it must be recognised and applauded. It is only through the good outcomes and consequences which young people feel that they are able to learn and apply what they have learnt to future actions. Good, calm feelings are valued and appreciated, and connections need to be made to those things which have led to them.

PEACEFULNESS AND FEELING SAFE

Resistance, struggle and protest may only occur within a safe place (Grey 1996). She argues that the feelings of peacefulness which attend being in a safe place allow the individual to act upon those feelings of peace, and oppose repression and suffering. Resistance is a refusal to accept defeat born of an inner confidence which can only prevail where there is an overriding feeling of safety. Scott did possess the confidence to resist the pain of another probably because he had learnt from someone over a long period of time, 'four years', that it was possible to listen to another person's pain and not be overpowered by it and still maintain a closeness. The closeness he had felt and still felt with this teacher who was able to listen to him contributed to his belief in himself and what he could accomplish:

> I actually wanted to become in the form of some support worker with people, help people who have had experiences and stuff and use my experiences and… basically knowledge and everything to help other people.

Scott did show compassion, as we have already discovered. The compassion arose out of an inner peaceful assuredness and a desire for peace which had overcome any natural inclinations to retaliate or be confrontational. He exhibited the transforming power which is contained within a desire for reconciliation. Peacefulness here is a force which appears to allow closeness and reconciliation beyond expectations.

Boler (1999) expresses the idea that oppression can provide us with a highly developed capacity for feeling. The consequences of this can be inhibiting as it might logically exclude us from any form of public life. Equally, it may encourage us into the service of others as nurturers and lead to subservient roles in society. Scott does appear to see himself in terms of the help he is able to provide, and is concerned that if he had not experienced suffering, he would not be able to care for others. The creative conflict resolution which Boler (1999) describes is evident in Scott's story. As he dreams and envisions a transformed future, he is able to keep his dreams alive (Grey 1996).

Coral describes how her dreams are kept alive in the safe place she goes to. She listens to Eminem, and reflects on the way he is close to his daughter, just as she would want her own dad to be with her:

> ...I would just sit in my room and just listen to Eminem because he's so close to his daughter and he writes about her and sings about her and I used to wish that dad would just be like that with me...

Robinson (2008) defines and echoes this image of quiet acceptance as serenity. A derivative of peacefulness, serenity implies an acceptance of reality. This is embodied in the self and in the situation. Coral is clearly conversant with the reality of her situation. She is also fully aware of her part, and how her identity as a father's daughter remains unfulfilled. She is able to acknowledge her feelings of disappointment, but they appear to be softened as she considers the love shown by Eminem to his daughter. Her acceptance of her own loss allows her to be reconciled to herself, to recognise cheerfully the better circumstances of others and provide her with an opportunity to be forgiving.

PEACEFULNESS AND FORGIVENESS

Forgiveness would seem to act as a prerequisite to peacefulness (Mananzan et al. 1996). Chung (1996) describes the interplay of these emotions as she writes about a woman enslaved and sexually abused. 'From Soo-Beck we learn her legacy of survival, forgiveness, and acceptance. Her survival was her liberation. Her forgiveness was her best revenge, and her acceptance was her best resistance' (ibid., p.137). The quiet acceptance which Robinson (2008) defines as serenity seems to depend upon an ability to forgive:

It wasn't my fault, it wasn't my mum's fault...it was just the drink 'cos like, I have seen other people get violent on drink. (Rose)

When my mum had all that time to have...to have all the time she wants with me but she never took it...she pushed me out...so I'm not trying to get back at her or nothing... (Rose)

Rose talks about how she tries not to make her mum feel guilty about the past. This involves the avoidance of those things which she sees as upsetting for her mum. Talking to her mum about her suicidal thoughts when she was at her lowest point was not something she could consider then and even years later. Rose's acceptance that her mum did put her and her sister through 'quite a bit' and her apportioning no blame has led to a feeling of forgiveness and peaceful agreement with her mum. Their relationship is close now: 'it did get really close and it still is close...me and my mum we talk more and we just bond more...' The bonding is like a flowering of their relationship into an image of contentment, in which each has accepted new responsibilities and is happy to pursue and fulfil them without feeling any regret or guilt towards the other:

It was time for mum to be the mum and me to be the teenager... I have been able to be myself.

This transformation is poetically described by Chung who likens it to a kind of exorcism from the ghosts of rage, fear and helplessness, to bring 'our full womanhood to bloom like a lotus flower of wisdom from a mud of suffering' (1996, p.133). Rose's story reflects what King (1996) describes as the ability to calm down quarrels. The calmness of the present conceals Rose's struggles for self-determination.

She had gained strength and peace knowing that the suffering 'isn't going to be for ever'. But she had followed that course 'because I am getting my own life...going out more with my friends...my confidence was like building all the time'. The tremendous effort expended by Rose displays 'a mission of peace with justice which will result in a beautiful world, a new creation, no longer hostile' (Oduyoye 1996, p.163). Significantly, the power to struggle for transformation seems to have come to her partly through the help of another. The support worker whom she saw as someone who had taught her an important truth provided her with crucial direction:

> *I've got more confident because he said to me you shouldn't let anyone put you down and...and it has worked. It has really worked. If anyone puts me down I just say I don't care... I don't care what anyone else thinks...I've become myself.*

Rose's avoidance of confrontation and her willingness to shrug off the put-downs do not indicate a silent acceptance of abuse born of fear. Her position does not reflect acceptance due to disempowerment. On the contrary, Rose is clearly empowered as she expresses the strength and sustenance that she feels as she has gained a new freedom and identity (King 1996).

Acceptance appears to be closely linked to forgiveness, and as the connection is forged, a resultant tranquillity born of making the connection becomes evident. Acceptance of destructive influences, which erode a positive sense of identity, in a way which views them as things which can be forgiven may lead to empowerment and an inner peace. Young people can be assisted on the way through providing them with the permission to talk about their suffering and its causes. Acceptance can only be accomplished when there has been ample opportunity to explain, to reflect, to describe and to ponder with another the effects of domestic violence.

PEACEFULNESS AND RECONCILIATION

The interconnectedness of Rose's experiences with others is a powerful thread which appears to twist her in the direction of accepting a mutual interdependence which means that she still feels a reliance, dependence and responsibilities associated with others (Oakley and Jenkins 1996). Despite a growing sense of personal identity and autonomy, Rose continues to remain close to the members of her family. In a story filled with suffering of the acutest kind, Rose's survival was caught up in the survival of her mum and sister:

> In societies in which people live closely together in mutual dependence...life is precarious and people depend on each other for survival. Within some of these societies, anger seldom arises and aggression is rare. (Oakley and Jenkins 1996, p.299)

Each family member received help and support almost simultaneously, and Rose's anger dissipated as they learnt to survive together:

> ...then she (mum) got help from —, and my sister was going to —, ...like a counselling session...and my mum said to — about seeing me...

As Rose connects with her family and with the support worker, any anger she felt evaporates and the peace born of reconciliation prevails. She sees her treatment of her sister as 'really nasty', and tries to reconnect with her. Her wish to re-establish a non-aggressive relationship with her sister does occur:

> I'm trying to make up for it now...'cos like I try to be there for her. I'm really nice to her now and I don't very often fight with her, but me and her used to fight a lot...

A relatively peaceful connection had been created by Rose, and with it an understanding of the reasons for her aggression previously. These reasons had been dealt with:

> ...maybe it was because she was the only person I could take something out on, because I was always stuck at home with her and because I was so young.

It is likely that Rose's acknowledgement and understanding of her need to 'take something out' on someone led to her present position of rejecting the aggressive, hurtful behaviour of her past, and wanting to eradicate the fights. She had called a truce, acknowledging contritely that she needed to make the changes. She had been able to voice her anxieties. She had talked about her life. This process had liberated her desire for peace, and peacefulness had entered her most intimate relationships.

Reconciliation occurs when the young person has reasoned out in their mind and out loud an understanding which they can accept partially or wholly. The process of reconciliation is a gradual one, allowing the young person gradually to figure out and piece together the meaning of their experiences. Developing a young person's thinking would seem to depend on discussions around accepting and not accepting blame, according to their actions and the actions of others, and recognising the criteria for each. As they develop a truer picture of their lives, they may be able to find that they can become reconciled to what has happened, and view the part they have played with clarity and acceptance.

PEACEFULNESS AND PLAY

The human need for attachment is crucial and inescapable (Bellous 2008). The recovery from loss or trauma in a healthy way requires 'true companions' (ibid., p.197), based on a social interaction which demonstrates mutual respect and caring (Goleman 2005, p.84).

The peaceful consequences of these interactions can be felt as Coral played with her brothers:

> *I tried to play a game with them or something so that they couldn't hear anything.*

Karl also speaks of playing with other children when he was in the refuge, which distracted from worrying thoughts:

> *I started playing with the other children that was there…just ignored it (feeling scared).*

The playing with others distracted thoughts and feelings about what was going on, and created a kind of calm which was a way of dealing with the situation. The games were in stark contrast to the violence in the room downstairs or in the home that had been left behind. Coral and Karl had turned to playing to combat the injuries, the suffering and the aggression.

The emotional effect of witnessing violent events and living so close to violent events leads to feeling scared, having intrusive thoughts and experiencing other symptoms of distress (Oakley and Jenkins 1996). Distractions can be easily created by play but there needs to be a significant mental and emotional effort made if the distraction is to be effective. There would need to be a whole-hearted commitment to the play activity, particularly if the situation required the involvement of others. It is remarkable that the young people who engaged in these activities were able to overcome their own feelings of fear and anxiety to such an extent that they were able to control them and convey quite different emotions to others. The peacefulness which is created by young people as they pursue playful, recreational activities is remarkable because it is formed at a time when their lives are stained by violence:

> *I did like writing stories…my main thing was writing and reading…it kind of comforted me and it kind of released me… (Rose)*

> *Whenever I got angry or something or upset at something I started to draw… and lately I've been doing that quite a lot. (Scott)*

The young people had discovered activities that were calming and 'releasing'. Boler (1999) discusses the need to express feelings appropriately. Both Rose and Scott were immersed in emotional struggles of the acutest kind. Angry and upset, emotionally aroused by indescribable abuse, they found a means of exploration and a creative way of self-expression which was appropriate and effective. The discovery of these ways seems to have been personal and remained private and in some measure secretive. Rose wanted to disclaim the real meaning of her stories:

> ...you putting the pen to paper and no one had to know what was happening to you but you could write...that's the sort of things that I used to write about... children getting hurt...parents getting hurt but they didn't need, the teacher didn't need to know what was happening at home.

It appears that in order for the means of expression to work, it has to remain deeply personal and retain an idiosyncrasy which intrinsically enables it to nullify unwanted feelings. As children and young people are creative in their chosen activities it provides opportunities for them to find personal answers and satisfactions, which are heart-warming and fulfilling.

PEACEFULNESS AND GRATITUDE

The journey from abuse and suffering to safety and peace is described by Gottlieb (2003) as one of gratitude and acceptance. Gaining or losing our hold on gratitude, peacefulness, acceptance and compassion is dependent on whether or not we feel at one with ourselves (ibid., p.12). Coral describes her feelings now that her family has got away from the abuse:

> ...we might not have much stuff as what everyone else does and things but I'm happy like with what we do have, 'cos we started with nothing.

She expresses gratitude for what they have achieved. There is a feeling of satisfaction and acceptance of a situation which may not compare favourably with that of other people, but which is seen as enough. Coral is thankful because the family has moved from having 'nothing'. Apparently she is talking about material 'things', and yet there is a sense of other gains which are probably emotional. Happiness is mentioned here. Coral has 'worked on the human tendency to be satisfied', and feels gratitude, contentment and an accompanying sense of peace (Gottlieb 2003, p.19):

We've got a house now... it feels just like a home again.

Her home feels safe and provides an emotional solution to the suffering of the past. The homeliness of her life allows her to be content.

Home-making and feelings of safety which spring out of the efforts made to make a dwelling 'homely' would appear to have some bearing on alleviating the suffering of the past. Homes do not seem to need a total focus on material possessions. Emotional values are appreciated more, and work can probably be done to support home-making in the sense of rebuilding the feelings of safety which come from responding positively to family members, and strengthening emotional bonds and attachments.

PEACEFULNESS AND RESISTANCE TO EVIL

Gottlieb defines the finding of peace as being dependent upon actively resisting that which is known to be evil or destructively ignorant (2003, p.13). There can be little doubt that each of the young people have resisted and struggled against the evil of abuse. Terry describes this struggle most graphically:

My mum tried to make it so she could call the shots and the solicitor said you can't do that. And I went, 'Why can't she do it?' 'cos then she's the one losing out and he's (dad) getting away with everything...

Terry challenges the possibility of the continuation of abuse. The unfairness and the injustice are not tolerated by him:

That's my dad wanted to control me. I wouldn't give it to him 'cos he's not winning. I don't care if I get told off or anything as long as he's not winning...

The struggle is a kind of combat where there are winners and losers. For Terry there can be no chance of his dad 'winning'. For his own peace of mind, he has to fight this battle, and not allow anything to deter him from 'standing up' to his dad:

I didn't really have any respect for him anymore. I did have a little bit but I don't have any respect for him anymore.

The personal connection with his dad has been severed. He did this because he recognised that his dad had continued to be abusive towards his sister as well as his mum. This abuse Terry found very disturbing:

This guy goes 'How many kids have you got?' and he (dad) goes three sons and I went 'You've got a daughter too', and he goes 'No I ain't'. You've got a daughter. And her name's — ain't it? That really hurt me. He pretended he didn't know her but thought it was a joke but it wasn't funny. He used to always do stuff like that…don't do it about your own family.

The connections are made to the past, and a recognition that what is happening cannot be accepted and must be resisted and overturned. There is a feeling that through Terry's courageous opposition to what he feels is unjust and unacceptable, he will ultimately acquire an inner peacefulness due to his having opposed injustice and abuse. Dorr (1990) describes this endeavour as possessing a keen sense of suffering which is unjustly inflicted. He adds that integrity and openness are evidence of a desire to make peace with others, and also a predisposition to challenge without resorting to violence:

If I stand up for myself, he'll (dad) go, 'What are you doing?' I go, 'Standing up for myself.' (Terry)

…he (dad) expects just us to sit down and listen. I won't. (Terry)

A refusal to accept circumstances and act in a way which decries what is happening indicates that Terry possesses the courage to question the rightness of his dad's behaviour. He seems to be measuring it with a moral 'yardstick' of his own making. He is able to assert his opinions by 'standing up for himself' which satisfies his yearning for justice. Peacefulness comes after the suffering is vanquished, and the person's dignity, self-respect and autonomy are enhanced (Robinson 2008).

Finally, there are examples of when the young people recognised the inappropriate occasions when it would have been wrong to resist the oppression:

I wanted to help (mum) but then if I did it would make things worse. (Coral)

…I felt I could (do something about the violence) but there was something holding me back like…fear or something. (Scott)

Unsure as to the real reasons for his unwillingness to intervene in what was happening, although it could have been fear, Scott still felt the urge to help, as did Coral. However, they both addressed the root cause of the problem and recognised that there were no benefits to getting involved in the violence at that time (Mananzan *et al.* 1996). The time for resistance was yet to come. The avoidance of violence reflects an embryonic desire to maintain a non-aggressive stance. The seeds of non-violent protest may be laid at this point, as the young people remain constant to the feeling that their violent responses to violence and abuse would not have a desirable outcome.

As the conclusion of these reflections of the emotionality within the young people's stories has come, I am reminded of Burstow's assessment of our vision as being 'limited' and regrets associated with possible misrepresentation or insensitivity (1992, p.xviii). At the start of my search, I knew that I would most probably need to be corrected. However, those who have been subordinated and silenced in the past do now possess an 'explicit discourse of emotions (which) will lead us to develop a meta-discourse about the significance of different emotional expressions...' (Boler 1999, p.82). It was important that the young people would remain central, as so much is to be gained in understanding the complexity of each individual young person by focusing on just a few, and for this end, their subordinated voices should be explicit and clear. However, as we approach each young person, being aware of the complexity of their emotions, we can apply some of the principles advocated here, knowing that there is a possibility that they may lead to emotional healing.

Concluding: depths of emotionality

The emotional expressions of the young people have been viewed in terms of specific emotions which I have described as disempowering or empowering, and their voices as being suffering or healing. Their emotional journey through their suffering has been directed at six specific emotions. However, the stories have revealed many other emotions, entangled and juxtaposed within them. I hope that the reader will have gained an insight into the journeys through suffering where, for example, compassion exists alongside aggression, where hopefulness may reside within fearfulness and where peacefulness might be found beside bitterness. The complexity of individuals' lives and the depths of emotionality have become clear.

Applying what we have learnt to voices of other children and young people needs to be considered here. Listening with an 'emotional' ear is where we probably need to begin. This is supported by the view that there seems to be little understanding of mental health difficulties experienced by children and young people by their parents and that teachers need further training as they are often consulted by parents in relation to their children's behaviour and emotional wellbeing (Loades and Mastroyannopoulou 2010).

The intrinsic value of every emotion and its voice is completely supported here. However, it is apparent that some emotions can be damaging to the wellbeing of a child if managed ineffectively or inappropriately. Care must be taken to balance the need to voice all emotions and the need to recognise that some need to change. How the changes come about is dependent upon how the balance is handled, and how a child can come to recognise the need for change.

The five young people show that their paths through their emotionality were completely within their control, and that the needed changes took place with their understanding and through providing them with the emotional tools to move in fresh directions.

The emotional wellbeing of these and any other young people exposed to domestic violence depends on the sensitive acknowledgement of their emotions, and an understanding that young people have it within their power to recognise the need for change and the capacity to effect it with the support of someone who can indicate the choices which may be available, and the encouragement which she or he needs.

It is my belief that very little can be accomplished without a thorough understanding of the emotional self of each child and young person. Without this understanding there is only a very small possibility that the young person can be supported effectively. 'How did that make you feel?' is a question that needs to be asked time and time again, and the answers need to be reflected upon and every effort made to come to some sort of understanding of the young person's emotional journey.

CHAPTER 4

Competency in Coping

To cope means to deal with something effectively. The relatively subjective nature of effectiveness makes an analysis of coping complex and at times seemingly contradictory. Coping may indicate an ability to manage, or it may mean just 'getting by'. It may be seen as surviving, which implies a kind of battle or struggle, or, in contrast, it may be defined as the capacity to hold one's own and to remain independent of outside forces. These examples of coping may exist in one person's life and may vary according to their effectiveness or competence.

It is clear that each individual possesses an individual capacity to cope with adversity, and each has a personal aptitude to thrive. My experience has been that some children appear to cope without any obvious signs of difficulty. In other words, they seem able to 'ride above' what is happening, and appear to be unscathed. However, some develop strategies which assist them in coping, and these are of particular interest as they may point to what needs to be encouraged, assisting the young person in forming positive patterns of behaviour which will of themselves help them surface above the dreadful experiences of their lives. It is mainly for this reason that the coping strategies are pinpointed and analysed.

As the consideration of the young people's stories of coping strategies unfolded, there needed to be an awareness of the complexities inherent in a study such as this. An overall view of coping might assist in the analysis of the young people's stories and so it is defined here as, first, 'an attempt to manage or deal with thoughts, feelings and bodily reactions under conditions of stress' (Murgatroyd and Woolfe 1982, p.22) and, second, 'changing a situation which is stressful' (ibid., p.22). Whether or not the attempts and changes are successful is not an intrinsic part of coping. Coping competency does, however, point to the degree of change or management achieved, and is dependent upon the individual's biography, make-up and relationships (ibid., p.25).

The competence with which children and young people cope with adversity and emotional trauma varies (Campion 1992). As was pointed out earlier, it would seem that some cope alright while others who have been exposed to violence and adversity display an impairment of emotional growth and stability. It is therefore necessary to examine the young people's ways of coping within the context of the abuse and then to focus on the aftermath, once the direct experiences of abuse have ended. This is founded on the idea that the abuse's effects may be long-lasting and require ways of coping long after the experiences of domestic violence have ceased. 'Children might experience a wide range of behavioural, physical and psychological effects, which may be short and/or long term (Hester *et al.* 2007, p.86).

It is also necessary at this point to emphasise 'the range of complex strategies of coping and survival' which are developed by children in order to deal with their experiences of stress and adversity (ibid., p.86). A strategy is a scheme adopted to cope, whilst a tactic is a person's way of implementing the strategy (Murgatroyd and Woolfe 1982). Coping tactics may include drinking alcohol, prayer, cycling, talking to someone not involved or concentrating on work. Strategies may involve, for example, preventative action to prevent situations developing as stressful, or the creation of a 'buffer' between the person and the stressful environment, or the management of thoughts and feelings.

Pathways

Aviles, Anderson and Davila (2006) define what they call 'pathways' which support children and young people in becoming competent in ways of coping, and these in some measure mirror the ideas of Grotberg (1997), Hague *et al.* (2002) and Sharp and Cowie (1998) who lay emphasis upon the encouragement of autonomy, the development and implementation of personal strengths and the presence of significant relationships. The purpose here is to look at the experiences of the young people and examine any evidence which supports the idea that the 'pathways' are described and/or implemented by the young people themselves.

There are five pathways described by Aviles *et al.* (2006) which can be used to structure and underpin the view of all young people's stories in the way described. These pathways to competence can be applied both negatively and positively in that they define competency in coping with adversity and what it is not. An assumption is therefore that the absence of any or all of the 'pathways' would indicate a low level of evidence to support competency in coping with adverse experiences. Again, the analysis begins with the young people's stories of the abuse and how they coped at the time, but also encompasses later ways of coping.

First pathway: cooperative behaviour

First, cooperative and pro-social behaviour, if encouraged, may assist a young person in becoming competent in how they cope with adversity and suffering. Positive social behaviour became important to Scott.

> ...at times when people are being mean towards each other or mean towards me...I'm polite back.

> There was a time when my friend was being nasty to me and I helped him out.

> We've done a group before and I was helping out with some of the people as well.

> Church has also been helping me...they pray and stuff...talk to me about things. It's like one big happy family.

The social behaviour described is based upon a desire for closeness to others which overrides unkindness and experiences of abuse. This pathway to coping is established through a refusal to adopt an antisocial stance, and a commitment to a view of other people which embraces the idea of interdependency. It is of particular interest that Scott established the idea of church as being like a 'family' when his own had been fraught with suffering and unhappiness. The potential for a family to be happy had never been completely discarded by him. The modification of Scott's understanding of social behaviour from the time that he abused his mother, thinking that it was 'right', to the time of the interview had been dramatic. He had consciously made some changes because of a realisation that something about him was 'silly'. His thinking about himself in relation to other people became a preoccupation which demanded a more intelligent approach. The silliness had to be swept away and replaced by attributes which he proudly noted were impressive to others:

> I decided I'm going to change now, because this is a bit silly and lately I've been getting really well... —'s impressed. All my support workers are very impressed.

Making an impression socially and impressing others who are seen in a favourable light has led to a degree of coping which sees the past experiences of suffering as a strength. Scott was able to recognise that his experience could be utilised and applied to others' experience for their benefit:

I picked up a lot of skills what people do…when I started to help my friends.

Cooperation with others using past experience as a conduit to assist and support him had led to an emotional plateau where problems can be overcome and where self-esteem is recognised and elevated. This supports the assertion made by Spielberger, Borucki and Sarason that 'an important factor in resistance to stress is a high level of self esteem' (1991, p.289).

Underpinning Scott's actions are his attitudes and his thinking which are founded on a realisation that he has to change. An inner awakening to the wrongfulness of what he had become, and his desire to be worthy of others' respect, had set him on the 'pathway' to pro-social behaviour. His good feelings had reinforced the 'pathway':

It felt really good.

Scott continues to apply his thinking to reaching out to other people. He became aware of how he had coped using aggression, and how that way of coping had to change. Once he had acknowledged this, he describes the new 'pathway' and how he got there:

…my mental strengths…probably…sometimes my sense of humour.

I think it's my attitude, it's made a difference and also how I think and how I act now. Lately because I used to be as — would say a P.I.T.A., a pain in the— (laughs), because I wasn't really nice towards my family, and school was really rubbish and I wasn't being nice towards my teachers, but lately my attitude has been changing, so…it's been good.

When I started to help my friends – I thought, I'm pretty good at this…

Pro-social behaviour had brought a reward in the way he was feeling, and had been instrumental in establishing a way to a better means of coping.

It appears to be evident that encouragement of social interaction and activity may lead to a degree of coping competency which has not been present before. This lends support to those actions by professionals who try to involve vulnerable children and young people in physical activities which demand group interaction and team building. This approach to finding ways of stimulating pro-social behaviour has proved beneficial for many young people. Programmes which focus on these elements may well lead to an increased capacity to cope with suffering and injury, and an improvement in resilience. Of course, this kind of activity may do much to increase self-confidence and emotional wellbeing. However, as cooperative relationships have been so prevalent in the shared stories, and I have no reason to doubt that this may well be a general trend amongst young people, there would appear to be a direct link to coping competency, and I would support the need to increase contacts with other interested or empathic individuals which would readily lend itself to the development of cooperative behaviour.

Second pathway: peer friendships/ adult relationships

A second pathway suggested by Aviles *et al.* (2006), which if followed will develop coping competency, is the initiation and maintenance of peer friendships and adult relationships:

I did speak to one of my friends...we kind of related really good and my mum and her mum were good friends...it was just nice to know someone was there, you know what I mean? (Rose)

...me and my mum we talk more and we just bond more... (Rose)

Rose demonstrates the closeness of specific relationships which are pivotal to her wellbeing and ability to cope with adversity. Friends and 'good friends' can be associated with what she describes as a 'bond', which is a kind of adhesion which maintains the relationship. The grip which bonds her to her mother and to her friend was a belief that they were 'there' for her. Being 'there' has connotations which imply a link which does not totally depend upon circumstances, but is more about a deeper, shared understanding. This may be the trigger which initiates and ultimately maintains the closeness of the relationship.

When Terry was asked if there was anything that had helped him he replied, 'Yes, me and my sister's boyfriend. He's been a lot of help 'cos he, he was in worse than me. And he's been talking to us every time we was upset or he's there...' The initiation of Terry's friendship was brought about by his sister's boyfriend 'being there' in an emotional as well as a physical sense. The maintenance of this relationship was a natural consequence of a bond built on an empathic understanding and acceptance. At times of upset, an emotional power appears to have been unleashed within the relationship which calms and supports and which provides a degree of coping competence which had been explicitly absent before:

He says everything is gone. All the stress is gone…and then we are not upset.

One relationship which Coral depended upon to the exclusion of all others while the abuse was going on was her relationship with her mother:

I thought I'd be speaking to my mum, and I didn't think I needed to speak to anyone else.

The closeness between mother and daughter is very clear, and Coral devoted herself entirely to building the relationship. It was later, once they had left Coral's dad, that the opportunity was provided for Coral to talk with a support worker:

I think she (mum) thinks that I didn't talk to her about everything… I didn't want to always talk about it because I was scared I would make her upset.

Coral's sensitivity to her mum's emotional needs indicates a very strong need to maintain the closeness of their relationship, and a continued affirmation of their interconnectedness. Nothing, if she could help it, would upset what they had. Coping through the maintenance of her closeness with her mum is evident, and this is what has sustained her through the suffering and afterwards. Later, she is able to initiate a particular friendship subsequent to their leaving to go into a refuge:

…then I met my friend now, my best friend and I can talk to her about nearly anything… I say to her all the time that if she needs to talk she can but… I think she's worried.

The sensitivity she felt in relation to her mum is apparent in the building of a new relationship which appears to provide a means of coping with the long-term effects of domestic violence. She believes that what has brought them together and maintained their relationship has something to do with her past experiences in relation to her dad. Her friend has 'problems' with her dad and Coral has shared her past because of a strongly held belief that experiences can 'help' others:

I want to talk about and hopefully let it help other people.

Each of these young people have valued and nurtured relationships with their peers and significant adults, and these have developed and been sustaining, revealing their significant contribution in assisting the young people in coping during and after their experiences of domestic violence.

I do not feel that the needs of these young people are dramatically different from those who have had similar experiences, in a general sense. Developing necessary social skills and self-confidence is probably a requirement for this coping pathway, and some, like Terry, would not seek out such relationships because of an impulse to withdraw and remain at the victim's side. As we reflect on the relationships which young people have and desire, an awareness needs to be recognised of the importance of the kind of relationship which is developed through a desire to help and strengthen a young person without a feeling of patronisation. Opportunities for young people may be sparse, and there will need to be some thought given to exposing the young person to a variety of experiences and contexts.

Third pathway: management of aggression

The third pathway described by Aviles *et al.* (2006) to increase competence in coping with suffering, abuse and exposure to violence is management of aggression and conflict.

Management can mean being able to cope with difficulties, implying a form of control which is self-induced. Managing aggressive feelings and conflict may be the result of applying what Cole, Martin and Dennis define as 'maladaptive strategies' (2004, p.329). This implies that the management may not be entirely contributory to the person's wellbeing, but may serve as the only means of coping seemingly available to the person at the time.

Aggressive feelings followed by actions have been analysed already, and have indicated the complexity of motivations surrounding aggressiveness. Expressions are clearly unique to the individual. Each young person described being hurt, followed by the ways each had found to hurt back (Ridgway 1973) or to internalise the hurt or to express the hurt in some other way. All demonstrate ways of coping which vary according to the degree the emotion of aggressive anger is managed:

He says, 'You're a donkey.' I go, 'You're a donkey.' That's what I do anyway. (Terry)

…we had like a huge argument, a lot of crying and screaming in the middle of the street, so… (Coral)

So I don't speak to him anymore…he doesn't really care. (Terry)

I don't know why I'd just get really angry with her (sister) really quickly and I'd just shout at her. (Rose)

…Because I wasn't really nice towards my family…and I wasn't being nice towards my teachers… (Scott)

I was going through a stage of self-harming…slitting my wrists and things like that, but I don't…it wasn't properly or nothing. (Rose)

The expressions of aggressiveness are sometimes directed at the perpetrator, sometimes at an innocent person, or sometimes at the person her/himself; they can be echoes of the original hurt or they may redirect or stifle the hurt in some way, and respond with hurtful silence. The difficulty lies in knowing whether or not the control or management exists and if so where it begins.

It would seem to be true that those young people who chose silence rather than aggressive retaliation exhibit an essential management of aggression which does nothing to perpetuate conflict. How they came to this point of non-aggressive action requires further analysis. Additionally, it is difficult to ascertain whether this way of coping is in any way potentially less harmful to the emotional wellbeing than overt acts of aggression as anger is expressed in, for example, the activity of boxing. As levels of emotionality reveal themselves, it may be difficult to judge or determine what is fundamentally a higher level or more efficacious way of coping competency:

He (brother) tries to fight…I just push him over. I don't see the point of hitting him…what we're doing now is…it doesn't hurt us…it's keeping us out of trouble and we're playing but we're doing like boxing and wrestling…just get our energy away from fighting. (Terry)

This aspect of coping is openly acknowledged by Terry as being a measure which is designed to divert aggressiveness into an activity which he and his brother enjoy:

He loves wrestling, I love boxing. We both want to be...my brother wants to be a wrestler and I want to be a boxer when I'm older...so we do that.

The 'energy' which fuels the conflict is adapted but also maintained. The emotion is not changed, but motivates a different course of action which is viewed as morally more acceptable. Aggression finds expression in a regulated way.

Scott's story is perhaps the most significant in this area. The change which took place was situated in a cognitive sense and was a change in the way he thought of himself. Prior to this he had been abusing his mother in particular and had been 'harsh' towards the other members of his family. The management of his aggression was facilitated by a situation which provided him with the means to ponder long and hard about what he was doing and who he was. He then made a conscious effort to change. It is a truly remarkable turnaround which seems to have been triggered by his arrest. It seems that Scott's experience supports the words of Hamlet: 'There's nothing, either good or bad, but thinking makes it so' (cited by Graham 2005, p.57).

Scott exhibited few emotional difficulties at the time of the interview. His coping competency in relation to his suffering and exposure to violence showed no distinctive impairment except in relation to his learning. He admits that his life at school in relation to his work is problematic:

A lot of teachers don't like me. My grades aren't too good...

Scott was able to inhibit his aggression towards his family and his peers through cognitive means. His thinking and learning seem to be focused on this aspect of his life, because he sees his close relationships as the most important part of his life. The management of the emotions which had led to abuse against his family would need to be assigned significant effort and energy, and he sees his faith as part of this:

I think I cope by staking in there basically, having faith and stuff because I am a Christian. So I pray and stuff like that about things.

Effort directed away from aggression towards faith, prayer and family indicates a multi-dimensional future which has evolved out of Scott's creative use of learning (Park 1999, p.19). It is interesting to note that Scott uses the word 'staking' when 'sticking' seems more appropriate. It may be a slip but it would be expected that a correction would follow if that was the case. Scott does not correct himself. To 'stake' sounds like to support and to strengthen. Scott copes through supporting and strengthening himself, and this seems entirely feasible when he follows up this remark by adding his commitment to an inner faith and spirituality.

His use of a spiritual means of coping with angry feelings requires further interpretation and understanding. As a development of ideas around interrogation of the self and of personal experience, there seems to be a connection between faith and the idea of 'Being' (Kane 1997). 'We feel we are at one with Being and are tapping into a source of vigour and connectedness. We may have the sense that we have not been abandoned' (ibid., p.5). Faith can be the source of meaning and courage, the fulfilment of the wish to 'stake in there'. The connectedness between hope and faith can be demonstrated. 'Hope comes of faith, for without faith, there is not hope…the things we hope for lead us to faith' (Uchtdorf 2008, pp.23–24). Young people can, through faith 'come to know, as inner experience, their unity with all other human beings. These are the sources of hope that may provide the courage and strength to shoulder full human responsibility' (Kane 1997, p.8).

Using spirituality as a coping strategy or 'tactic' (Bone 2008, p.270) to overcome aggressive feelings and actions does appear to connect with the young people's hopeful pronouncements which have been discussed in the section entitled 'humanising emotions'. Scott's simple pronouncement 'I'm going to change now' expresses a belief and a hopefulness that change is entirely possible as well as a concurrent self-belief in his ability to accomplish it. It also expresses an intrinsic desire to change, which is urgently required 'now'. The need for change has been contemplated and decided upon without reservation, and the decision appears to be based upon an optimism and hopefulness which is grounded in faith. Faith seems to be the key to making the decision to change, and cope with his past aggression and anger. Bone (2008) describes this process as a tactic as opposed to a strategy, which she proposes allows people to make sense of the situation they are in. 'I propose spirituality as the ultimate "tactic"…recovery and healing is possible when certain "tactics" succeed and there is a sense again of wholeness, empowerment and joy' (ibid., p.270).

As young people find ways to manage their feelings of aggression and avert conflict, they demonstrate depths of understanding and spirituality which resolve into the development of a coping competency which clearly reflects their inner strengths and abilities. We would do well to view the ways that young people overcome feelings of revenge and aggression, and wonder at their ability to feel untroubled by suffering and injustice.

Instilling hope in the minds and hearts of those we come into contact with is something we should desire. Perhaps we can rejoice with those we nurture, knowing that conflict and contention can be neutralised by our gentle encouragement to believe in a light at the end of the tunnel. As one young person who had been part of the Cheshire Domestic Violence Outreach Service said, she had decided to work hard at school so that she could get her exams now that she had a hopeful instead of a pessimistic vision of the future. This comprehensive service had provided support for her and other children and their mothers since 2001, offering a wide range of services appropriate to their need. This kind of service needs to be available to all children and young people and their mothers (Cheshire Domestic Abuse Partnership 2005).

Fourth pathway: self–mastery and self–worth

The development of self-mastery and self-worth is the next 'pathway' which leads to a greater competence in dealing with adversity. Seligman co-joins self-mastery with optimism and asserts that the acquisition of these attributes will ensure the banishment of helplessness and depression (2007, p.8). This fourth pathway implies a personal struggle which is dependent upon an individual's own resources and this must partly be the case.

However, the stories of the young people appear to indicate that significant people in their lives were able to foster self-mastery and self-worth in the young people in sensitive and specific ways. Mastery implies self-discipline and a strength directed towards control. Boler writes of this as 'I am in control of me' (1999, p.91) and goes on to describe those educational 'emotional intelligence' programmes (Goleman 1995), which have been designed to facilitate emotional and social development. An underlying principle of all the programmes appears to be the apportioning of blame to those who have difficulty controlling themselves. Mastery of personal emotionality, thinking and behaviour is a universal virtue which the programme encourages. In the context of individual young people who possess the complex uniqueness of culture, family and experiential diversity and opportunities, perhaps mastery needs to be viewed differently:

I was allowed to be me for once. I was allowed to be myself. I didn't have to worry about what was going to happen as I walked through the front door... I started going out with my friends more and they were showing me different things...how to be... (Rose)

The kind of mastery exhibited here is wrapped up in a sense of being and of self. Rose was recognising her own needs along with sensing her own uniqueness. The comfortable feeling which she experienced as she began to recognise herself and know that she could accept herself and just be herself expanded into a more general sense of wellbeing and self expression:

...it was kind of confidence from my friends plus – and my confidence was just building up all the time.

Self-recognition is overcoming those influences which disallow a young person from expressing their uniqueness. Giving permission to young people is a significant step in their being able to gain mastery as an individual and gain a feeling of self-worth:

That's my dad wanted to control me. I wouldn't give it to him 'cos he's not winning. (Terry)

I don't care if I get told off or anything as long as he's not winning and he's realised now that if he talks down to me, I'll talk down to him...he's starting to talk with more respect to me. (Terry)

The echo of Terry's belief in his self-worth is clearly expressed here. As he responds to the emotional abuse of his dad he displays a willingness to assert his personal rights. He shows this awareness through his recognition of himself and his needs, and the strength and courage to 'stand up for himself':

My dad didn't like anyone who stands up for himself. If I stand up for myself he'll go, 'What are you doing?' I go, 'Standing up for myself.'

This way of coping had been passed on to him by his sister's boyfriend. The result of the experiences with him and later with his dad had been an increase in self-mastery and self-worth:

'Cos he's (sister's boyfriend) told me what to do and how to do it. Don't take the crap. 'Cos you'll be missing out. Everyone...everyone in the world'll be thinking it, so you just can't take the crap.

Terry had such confidence in the advice to act in the way he had chosen that he believed that the 'world' would not be able to stop him. As his confidence and feelings of self-worth increased he was able to cope with his dad's emotionally abusive attitudes:

> *I don't have any respect for him anymore. I did have a little bit but I don't have respect for him anymore.*

The stories of the young people indicate the crucial element of the 'other' in building self-mastery and self-worth. Abuse tears down self-mastery and self-worth. It seems likely that the young people all needed support in the rebuilding of their self-worth, because their stories reveal that the building blocks were put into place by members of their family, friends and professional support workers.

Once again it is apparent that the building of positive relationships in order to form and encourage an improved self-mastery and self-worth is crucial and critical, and there is evidence to support that this results in an increased coping capacity. There is evidence to show that relationship programmes can have a marked effect. Bell and Stanley (2006) demonstrate that a Healthy Relationships programme showed that 'some young people were able to demonstrate that they had developed positive ideas about healthy relationships' (2006, p.237). Young people's access to such programmes would appear to be beneficial not only in relation to having a better understanding of what constitutes a healthy relationship, but would also assist them in recognising abusive relationships and gain a better understanding of domestic violence.

Fifth pathway: emotional regulation

The final pathway advocated by Aviles *et al.* (2006) is defined as emotional regulation. Bringing order, direction and control to emotional experience within well-defined rules would appear to be the requirement of regulation. Again, there does appear to be some form of connection to ideas associated with emotional intelligence (Goleman 1995). As Boler writes, 'The equation of emotional intelligence with self-control evidences the fact that the emotionally intelligent person is still the man of reason' (1999, p.61). The acquisition of emotional skills provide the means 'to express the right emotions in the right way' (ibid., p.61).

The construct 'emotion regulation' has warranted a diversity of opinion and view as to its meaning and application. Cole *et al.* (2004) open the debate by questioning whether emotions are regulated or regulating. In their view, the essence of emotion regulation lies in changes which appear to result from an activated emotion which they define as 'emotion as regulating'; or changes in the activated emotion which they define as 'emotion as regulated'. The changes are the critical factors and are fundamental to either process:

> *She (mum) used to call me her favourite...not her favourite...her magic boy, because when she was sad I knew exactly what to do...just smile and give her a hug and anything like that. (Terry)*

The 'magic' being talked about is Terry's willingness and ability to change his mum's emotional state from sadness to something quite different. This shows a change from a state of sadness into making an unhappy parent smile and demonstrates an emotion as regulated:

> *Most of the time I would just sit in my room and just listen to Eminem because he's so close to his daughter and he writes about her and sings about her and I used to just wish that dad would just be like that with me... (Coral)*

It appears that the regulating of the emotions associated with the experiences of domestic abuse and violence evolves from experiences which appear to be far removed from them. Coral removed herself physically from the abuse and went to her room. There she would dream of a different kind of life with a different kind of dad. The link with her dad was central to her chosen way of coping. The emotions which were associated with her dad appear to be dulled by a choice to associate with a different kind of dad, one who cared and loved his daughter. This example appears to illustrate an emotion as regulating, as Coral found this experience soothing.

The debate around emotion regulation was succinctly covered in the *Journal of Child Development* in 2004 (Vol.72, No.2). It is a complex construct which many have used 'as a tool to understand how emotions organize attention and activity and facilitate strategic, persistent or powerful actions to overcome obstacles, solve problems and maintain well-being' (Cole *et al.* 2004, p.318). Here the emphasis is on emotions as motivators. Cole *et al.* (2004) emphasise the focus of regulation as change. Others state that it should be defined in terms of control. However, the view of this analysis is that the young people demonstrate an emotion-related self-regulation which encompasses a vast range of coping tactics which involve initiating, avoiding, inhibiting, maintaining, modulating and adapting emotions in order to achieve personal goals. These may be based on hedonistic values which if implemented result in self-satisfaction and fulfilment (Park 1999).

At other times, the goals may reflect a preoccupation with the needs of others, which supports the importance of initiating and maintaining relationships. Larson does, however, highlight the central role of research in this area as a 'need to focus on what factors account for the largest downturns in emotional level in early adolescence and what can be done to avert them, as well as look for what factors promote lasting upturns in baseline emotional state' (2002, p.1162).

Spielberger et al. state, 'Multilevel studies of emotions are urgently needed to deepen our insights about the emotional process' (1991, p.61). The concept of many levels of emotionality has attracted my attention because of the apparent lack of relevant research. The 'lasting upturns' in emotional state spoken of by Larson (2002) are of particular interest. A further exploration and examination of others' efforts to achieve a multilevel analysis is needed.

Emotional intelligence has possessed a popularity and a following which is based upon the general acceptance of the benefits of 'mastery of emotions through biological potential for logical choice' (Boler 1999, p.75). This embraces the scientific view of a person as being 'an organism whose brain contains pre-designed neural pathways to learn social behaviours' (ibid., p.75). It is argued that an individual is able to acquire autonomy along with social and emotional skills. This is the ontological view contained within the dominant discourse of emotional intelligence.

However, the view here is different because ethically contained within a heuristic approach there is an imposition to see things differently, to challenge what is accepted and to examine assumptions and acquired ways of seeing which may constrain creative thinking. For this reason, the term 'emotional literacy' seems to embody a closer identification with this search for meaning. Park (1999) describes how emotional literacy seeks to deepen young people's self-understanding through talking and relating to others so forming 'links between inner worlds and their outer experience' (1999, p.24).

This is supported by a programme for young people that is designed to promote emotional resilience which connects the emotional state of 'calmness' with self-awareness. 'Calm brings peace to the heart and clarity to the mind. Calm people have self-awareness. They become more aware of themselves and their emotions' (Bellhouse, Fuller and Johnson 2005, p.4).

This view leads to the belief that the idiosyncratic coping with and management of emotion is based upon internal and external laws which have evolved through experience. Introspective regulation is a response to a process of interrogation of experience which leads to an understanding of personal power (Holland, Blair and Sheldon 1995), and a recognition of knowledge and creativity:

I didn't want to talk about it because I was scared I would make her (mum) upset and I was scared it might make her want to take him (dad) back. (Coral)

The knowledge that Coral had gained about her mother's relationships with her and her father had been grafted into her cognitive and emotional response. She knew that she held the power to recognise what needed to be done to avert disaster and her 'scared' feelings were cathartically instrumental in determining her actions.

This form of personal interrogation is empowering and self-fulfilling. Coral does not appear to have suffered any long-term emotional impairments due to her self-imposed silence. She had spoken to no one about her suffering. Her recognition of the moment when she needed to talk appears to be sudden, because again she knew what the circumstances had to be like, and she immediately embraced the right opportunity:

...didn't really want to talk to anyone about it...and now that it's all out and I've told — everything...I can move on...and try and put it in the past.

The emotional relief and release can be felt as Coral haltingly expressed how she had come to change her thinking and feeling and ultimately her actions, and this is echoed by Rose when she talks about her management of emotions through various chosen activities:

My school work was kind of a relief really...my main thing was writing and reading...it kind of comforted me and it kind of released me. You could write down what was happening to you but they wouldn't know that...

Coping with a recognised inner suffering requires the application of a source of comfort. Relief is an expiation of pain which Rose knew that she could accomplish through reading and writing. Her self-interrogation and creative expression of these emotions was dependent upon the sure knowledge that what she was doing was not understood by anyone.

Just as self-injuries are covered by sleeves, so Rose hid her pain in story writing and introspective reading.

The power of her personally-found solution was felt by Rose. She was released and relieved, and it was accomplished by her alone. Emotional interrogation might lead to the recognition that there existed unhelpful feelings which would need to be replaced by more helpful ones (Stallard *et al.* 2007):

> *I'd just get really angry with her (sister)... I was really nasty to her...now that I'm much older, I think it's really nasty the way I was towards her, but then I'm trying to make up for it now...*

The understanding of the need to modify her feelings towards her sister grew over time. Now that she was 'much older', Rose perceived her method of coping in the past as 'nasty'. The anger was in some way dissipated or redirected. She no longer needed to vent her aggressive feelings on her sister:

> *She was the closest thing I could have a go at.*

> *But it was quite nasty when I think about it now.*

Rose could not act directly upon those who had perpetrated the violence and abuse in her life. She coped by demonstrating the need to express her distress when her sister was 'close' to her. The 'closeness' of their relationship is a significant factor in Rose's coping actions. Now, she has an opportunity to right the wrong, because the closeness to her sister remains.

The concept of emotional regulation, whether it is defined as change or control, has been extended beyond the parameters of the individual to theories which are clearly more to do with how the individual is able to respond to the world. McCubbin *et al.* (1998) state that a sense of coherence is instrumental in a person's ability to mobilise resources that seem appropriate in order to cope. This sense is firmly based on an ability to see the world as ordered and structured so that sense can be made of it. The cognitive aspects of coherence are evident. The world is comprehensible and meaningful, and leads to coping which 'makes sense emotionally...one wishes to cope' (McCubbin *et al.* 1998, p.7). The wish to cope is crucial, and this is demonstrated by Coral when she reflects on how she sees her present in relation to the past:

> *Now that it's all out and I've told — everything, I feel that it's always going to be there but I can kind of move on...*

The desire to cope with suffering found expression in her willingness to talk to a support worker. It was through this effort that she was able to make sense of the past, and she was able to think herself free of those parts which had emotionally and psychologically held her back and prevented her from moving forward in her life. This acknowledgement of her world and her story shows that Coral was able to see her experience in coherent, consistent and convincing ways. Park (1999) states that young people need opportunities to understand their own history, and make sense of any painful experiences. By 'opening up experiences' each person can 'fathom the mysteries' of their lives (1999, p.28):

> *At first like I didn't really want to say anything but then throughout it I got like more confident and realised that it wouldn't be said unless its like it needs to be said like to my parents. (Karl)*

Karl had been very fearful that his dad would discover the family's whereabouts and had been very careful not to talk about the location of the refuge on the phone to his dad and this had been generalised into a pervading silence. 'Children living with domestic violence may keep silent about what they know or have observed and will disclose this information only when they are given permission to do so' (Hester *et al.* 2007, p.81). The fear had strangled him to the point that he 'didn't really want to say anything'. However, as he had been offered the opportunity to talk, he saw himself as growing in confidence and feeling safer.

Karl had literally 'opened up' (Park 1999), and despite his secrecy acting as a coping strategy in the past, he was able to cope more effectively with his past suffering as he made sense of his feelings and his experiences as he broke his silence:

> *When he (support worker) first walked in I was like, it's a man, and...I don't trust men after everything and, but he sat down and basically said, he basically showed me it was ok to talk... (Rose)*

Rose demonstrates the truth of this statement. The support worker had offered Rose the most essential piece of knowledge that it was alright to speak of her experiences. 'They need to express what they feel – however unpleasant or difficult it may be to listen' (Park 1999, p.28). Through talking there is an opportunity to find out, to compare experience, to explore at an emotional level. The richness of experience can be revealed and spiritual understanding may develop (ibid.).

The complexity of the young people's coping competency has been exposed, particularly in relation to their 'emotional burdens' (Newman 2004, p.23). There are multilevel interpretations which highlight the differing strategies and tactics employed by each of the young people as they coped with the domestic violence and abuse, their relationships, their loss of their homes and loved ones, their changes of circumstances, their feelings and all the consequences which accrued because of all of these factors.

Illustrations can be drawn from each of the stories of the young people. Karl applied an emotional buffer while in the refuge by involving himself in the activities organised by the support workers so that he could 'ignore' his scared feelings. His feelings of loss, of his home, his pets, his friends and his possessions, were managed through his refusal to see his dad, his open acceptance that his dad did not care, and the initiation and maintenance of a new friendship begun in the refuge. These provided Karl with enough emotional support to cope with his dad's abusive behaviour and the effects of the abuse and violence on the whole family. Additionally, Karl had had to change his school three times, had been forced to live in a refuge more than once for a few months and had lived in fear of his father finding out where they were living. He admitted that his relationship with his sister had been adversely affected by his dad's behaviour. It had somehow come between them, but he had learnt to accept that this was something he had no control over. He was worried about his younger brother being coerced by his dad into contact, but had coped by keeping close to his brother and influencing him that way. He had talked about his experiences when he was given the opportunity and 'permission' to do so, and he had learnt about trust and had become more confident as he reflected on how he had managed the adversity which had come into his life. His positive view of his family in the present is significant. This is based on new experiences with his step-dad which have been 'fun'. He describes his family optimistically:

I think like it's improved a lot.

Feelings of powerlessness, upset, anxiety and helplessness have been washed away by waves of support, friendships and optimism. The hopefulness encapsulated by an optimistic view is displayed, and a 'positive strength, a sunny but solid future-mindedness' (Seligman 2007, p.301) is revealed.

Concluding remarks

Each of the young people has employed coping strategies and tactics in a variety of ways. The framework provided by Aviles *et al.* (2006) has facilitated an analysis which has highlighted the significance of emotionality and socio-development. The richness and depth of the stories has led to an appreciation of the young people's capacities, emotional, cognitive, and spiritual. The 'waves' of support, provided by both external and internal influences, have been seen to wash away the adverse effects of domestic violence.

These 'waves' of support have become evident during the process of investigation into the competency of coping of each of the young people, using the framework provided by Aviles *et al.* (2006). Crucially, this framework relies upon elements of emotionality which have highlighted the overlapping nature of the previously discussed emotional journeys and the congruently placed coping pathways. The 'waves' appear to be largely dependent on the emotional resilience of each young person's inner journey, which in some measure are sourced and given impetus by significant 'others'.

The inner life of each young person is certainly influenced by relationships, but the complexity of these influences remains to be revealed.

The metaphor expressed here, comparing support to the washing away of the effects of suffering and abuse by 'waves', will be developed further. A recognition of the 'waves' of resilience brought about by internal and external influences may lead to the means whereby there might be a more thorough understanding of what young people need, as individuals, as they go through their struggles. We need to ask children and young people, 'What helped you when things were so difficult? How did you manage? When you felt upset what did you do?' As young people reflect on how they reacted, we receive an invaluable insight into what we might be able to provide or encourage, in order that a young person might cope more effectively, and be able to accept help when it is needed.

CHAPTER 5

Views of Relationships

Young people will share their stories with others when somehow the necessary trust for this to happen is achieved. Creating these relationships with interested adults, which the young people seek and value, provides an abundant opportunity for them to talk about a part of their lives which seems to hold a major interest for them, their relationships. It is my experience that their storied 'facebooks' enjoy the forefront of their thinking, and as such reveal an enormous range of thoughts and feelings. Anything related to their family, friends, teachers and others grabs their attention, and is central to their lives.

We have already discovered the way relationships creep into many aspects of young people's lives. Chronologies, emotions, coping and identity have possessed connections with relationships which have intensified their critical nature, and have revealed a map of suffering which centres on those significant individuals who have exacerbated or relieved the suffering. Surprisingly, those who have been ineffectual have also been remembered and described. Young people appear to have a distinctive leaning towards what all other people are doing, saying, thinking and feeling. As they are forming their own views of the world around them, they seem to readily glean what they can from everyone around them and absorb or repel what they experience. The stories of the five young people reflect this preoccupation vividly, but also reveal a graduation of response which we all need to be aware of.

The views which have been expressed by each of the young people, and which embrace each young person's ideas and perceptions of their relationships, form a significant theme which encompasses how each young person looked out from beyond the confines of themselves and made connections, bonds and attachments with other people.

Relationships have already been identified as playing a part in building pathways to coping competency. This theme also encompasses each young person's emotional journey, as so much of this aspect of their stories was entwined with and enmeshed in their relationships. Here the 'waves of resilience', described at the conclusion of the previous chapter on coping competency, appear to spring out of significant relationships and are dependent upon the views held by the young person and the 'other'. What those of us who are engaged in supporting children and young people need to remember is that the kind of relationship which may or may not be helpful is entirely dependent on the contribution we make:

> The right thing to do is risk one's own comfort for the sake of another's freedom. (Boler 1999, p.196)

The purpose of this focus on relationships is to address in some measure the overwhelming need to understand how those of us who wish to be supportive can encourage and facilitate young people in the making of connections, and what conditions allow this to happen. To some extent this awareness can come through the examination and analysis of the conditions which prevailed in the lives of the young people who shared their stories. As we explore their relationships and seek to peel away any distractions which divert us from fully immersing ourselves in their voiced attachments, we may be able to decipher how the relationships become significant, and what we might need to consider as we support other young people.

The stories of the young people displayed a wide variety of ways that they had positively connected with various other significant people. From their point of view, the connection had, for the most part, led to a relief of suffering; for those who had responded to their needs, there was a definite risk to their own comfort which they had chosen to ignore. The 'freedom' felt by the young people brought on by those who had been willing to take the risk was deeply felt and appreciated:

> ...the person who gave me that idea was my auntie...'cos she knew everything that was going on and she always said to me, she said once you're old enough you can do whatever you want... (Rose)

Rose had held a 'picture' in her mind which she 'looked at'. This was given to her by her auntie, and it was such a strong influence that she had held it for many years since she was 'small', the idea that she could at some future time 'leave' the life which had brought her so much unhappiness and uncertainty. Little is said about the auntie except that she was 'the person' and that she had a thorough understanding of what Rose was living through. She also possessed the capacity to create within Rose the idea of a life which could be very different from the one she had known. It was just what Rose needed to know.

A new view of her life was presented to her that she clung to and hoped for. She had looked to her auntie and her auntie had presented her with a totally wonderful and powerful reality which could be hers and which could eradicate hopelessness and helplessness. This view undoubtedly contributed to Rose's healing voice as she embraced the idea that she possessed the ability to change her life. Her preparations for that moment demanded that she should look to others who might assist her, and so she sought out people who would strengthen her resolve and who would build her confidence:

> ...it was kind of confidence from my friends plus — and my confidence was just like building up all the time.

> ...he said to me it's ok to be myself, it's ok to be a teenager...he said to me you shouldn't let anyone put you down.

Rose's view of those around her had evolved from a realisation that she could escape her suffering. She recognised that she would need help but was sufficiently aware of her own needs to look to the right sources for that help:

> Secure attachment relationships in the family...facilitate the development of well-organized and flexible internal representations of self in relation to others. (Sharp and Cowie 1998, p.7)

The young people's stories do demonstrate attachments in their families which appear to be both secure and insecure. However, it is unclear sometimes how the young people view their mothers in particular. Each appears to struggle with knowing how to see their mother, which is hardly surprising as each was trying to see beyond the abuse to get a picture of their mother which would be free of pain:

> I don't think that...she's a bad mum or anything...

I thought I'd be speaking to my mum, and I didn't think I needed to speak to anyone else.

...I've come to like them 'cos she's friends with my mum.

...my mum's scared and so was I...

Their identification with their mothers, having empathy with them, supporting them, valuing what they value and seeing them as absolutely essential to their wellbeing, supports the importance of a strong view of their mothers which refuses to allow them to be discredited. Despite their mothers being unable at times to meet the needs of their children, they are generally viewed with compassion.

The relationships between the mothers and the young people have been beset by abusive intrusions and upheavals which have unsettled them and caused confusion within the family. In consequence, the relationships are not 'typical' in the accepted sense, but are fraught with misunderstandings around the part each should play and how they should communicate with one another. The young people's view of their mothers demands a response which is outside what generally would be expected:

...mum was the child and I was the adult... I've still got that adult instinct in me but I always will have because I've had that since I was five.

She was like a lot more dressier and that.

I'd been acting very adult like to survive and things...

I was using abuse towards my mum... I was not proud of that...

She'll be safe 'cos I know I can defend her.

The needs of mothers and the view they have of their children affects the way young people see them in complex ways. The stories have highlighted the words of Hester *et al.* which describe the effects of loss. 'Research has shown that women who experience domestic violence suffer immense social, economic, emotional and psychological losses. These may include the loss of safety and security, loss of physical health and emotional wellbeing, and loss of self, love, faith in the possibility of change and confidence in the future' (2007, p.252). The 'bereavement' of their mothers was experienced by their children also:

...when my mum first got rid of —, it was really depressing because mum was so depressed...she just wanted to drink all the time...

...she'd left before and gone back with him.

I didn't want always to talk about it because I was scared I would make her upset...

...we missed dad so mum started to try and get us to have contact with him... so she would drop us off...but then he would always get in the car with her and tell me to go into my auntie's house...

Refuge life in relation to their mothers reveals unspoken pressures which result in a widening of relationships. The stories describe a fragmentation of family life generally which is systematic of the first phase of bereavement which comprises 'feelings of shock, numbness, confusion, unreality and grief' (Hester *et al.* 2007, p.253). Young people's views of their mothers are complicated by having to live with other families:

It's not nice having to share like a house with loads of people and sometimes they weren't very nice people either...

*They **tried** to make it feel homely. (emphasis added)*

The effectiveness of support for women and their children in a refuge and beyond would seem to depend largely on an understanding of the losses that the woman has suffered and the grieving process. The effects these have on the relationships between children and their mothers, added to the effects of the domestic violence, demands a response to the needs of the mother and efforts to reverse the fragmentation of their relationship.

The stories of the young people did reveal an example of this kind of holistic support which was firmly structured to build the relationship between mother and daughter, along with persistent emotional support for the mother:

...then she (mum) got help from — (support worker)...then like — (support worker) started seeing me...and he said to me, that it's ok to be myself...and helping my mum at the same time get off the drink and just becoming a mum, not the child...it has worked... It has really worked...me and my mum we talk more and we just bond more... (Rose)

The stories raised the presence of other significant people in the lives of the young people. The view of fathers was generally dark and troubled, but remained clear and evident despite the violence and abuse perpetrated by them. The young people were very clear about how they perceived their fathers:

I hated my step-dad.

...I was upset because obviously I love my dad...but also he said he'd change before...and he changed like for two days and then he was back to his normal self. So I just knew that it was all an act. He wasn't going to change.

I don't have any respect for him anymore. I did have a little bit but I don't have respect for him anymore.

I don't speak to him anymore...he only sent two letters that's all. He doesn't really care.

The views of the young people indicate an understanding of their fathers which has been carefully framed beyond the bewilderment and confusion caused by the domestic violence. Judgements are made according to their experiences overall. Despite having to fend off his father from seriously hurting his mother, Terry had still allowed 'a little bit of respect' for his father to filter through. This had gone, however, when he felt there were no grounds for it. The view of each young person had distilled into a clear image of their fathers which they seem to say has come entirely from themselves.

Allowing children and young people to come to their own conclusions about their relationships with their fathers would uphold the right of every child and young person to be consulted in relation to contact arrangements. Their wishes and concerns must be considered, along with a process to carefully evaluate any attached risks, in order to safeguard every child and young person from harm.

The stories revealed some significant relationships beyond the immediate family. This, however, varied considerably between the young people. Where some describe extreme isolation at the time of the domestic violence where silence is maintained at school and friends do not exist, others speak of people who act in a significant way and who are valued by the young people.

Scott establishes closeness with a support worker, a teacher and a few friends at school. Karl finds friends in the refuge, and finds pleasure in activities with them. Coral has one 'best friend' whom she has got to know since leaving the refuge. Rose has 'friends and boyfriends' but again it seems that these relationships have been recently formed.

Terry tells of the closeness of his relationship with his sister's boyfriend, when other relationships are sometimes problematic as with his brother and a teacher. The sparseness of these relationships would appear to indicate their crucial and critical nature.

The stories have shown the strong link between coping competence and healthy relationships, relationships which are respectful, supportive and empathic. The importance of these through the eyes of the young people cannot be overestimated. The understanding and acceptance offered by this small group of people is a very significant part of each of their stories. The emotional journey of each was stabilised and enriched by these relationships, through their listening and offering hope and giving emotional strength based on a willingness to understand. The security offered by trusted 'others' provided the young people with the environment to freely express disempowering as well as humanising emotions, and with their support were able to make adjustments which resulted in the waning of the suffering voice, and its attendant emotions:

I think most of the support came from — (support worker) and I think that really helped me because I was keeping a lot of stuff inside.

Just knowing that he (support worker) was there to help...

He's (sister's boyfriend) been a lot of help...it's helped me a lot 'cos he's told me what to do and how to do it...and tells us what it's like when it's better...

Then I met my friend now and I can talk to her about nearly anything...

Think like he's (support worker) helped me a lot...better.

The views of the young people had shifted from uncertainty and distrust to acceptance and approval. This is particularly true in relation to the young women who had been supported by a male support worker. Deep layers of uneasiness were replaced by a realisation that all men are not like their fathers, and a willingness to trust and to acknowledge that 'there's other people out there that can help'.

As the stories of the young people unfolded, a clear picture of their widening views emerged, as respectful relationships surfaced whilst others less healthy dissolved. A greater certainty of relationships being helpful began to be discovered and embraced.

The stories show that offering young people opportunities to build mutually supportive relationships, and encouraging involvement from wider family members who care, would inevitably build a more positive connection with others, leading to the healing of emotional and psychological wounds created by perpetrators of domestic violence who have been indifferent to their suffering.

The instigation of 'waves of resilience' was initiated by the young people as they came into contact with others who inspired sufficient trust and empathy within the relationship. Each young person, except for possibly Coral and Rose, was prepared and ready to receive and use the 'waves' provided and the result had been beneficial. It is interesting to note that Coral and Rose are the two young women interviewed. At the time of interview they were 14 and 15 years old. For them, the relationship that had occupied their lives had been with their mothers, and on the whole they had not expected or sought support from them. However, the professional supportive relationships which emerged later were instigated by their mothers, and this is significant.

A further consideration must be given to the distortion of relationships by domestic violence, through the contorting of typical roles within the family, and the adverse effects caused to parenting ability and confidence. Children will sometimes become carers and will embrace adult responsibilities. Mothers will sometimes impose adult thinking and cares upon their children without being aware of the consequences of such action. Relationships are impacted by these behaviours, and the dynamics of the family may become atypical and corrosive.

It is evident from the stories of these young people that 'waves of resilience' which are significant in eroding the adverse effects of domestic violence are created by the views held by the young people in relation to trusted and empathic adults and peers. Once trust and empathy are established, 'waves of resilience' are created which literally buoy up the young person emotionally and psychologically and diffuse the pain created by abuse. An analysis of what creates trust is needed.

First, there is a need to be non-judgemental, creating a sense of safety and comfort, enabling honesty and openness to be present (Holland *et al.* 1995). Second, the demeanour of those who apparently possess greater power within a relationship, for example an adult or a professional adult, is crucial. There is a need to seek a feeling of equal status, to encourage a feeling that the adult is the learner (Alldred 1998). Third, empathic feelings need to be developed for those we want to trust us. Entering into the world of the child or young person, and immersing oneself in their feelings and thoughts, allows the possibility of becoming less controlling and more willing to follow their views and shifts of consciousness. This may lead to an empathic understanding (Ribbens and Edwards 1998). Using a non-judgemental approach and having a desire for equality and empathy, a child's feelings of trust may grow and allow a relationship to develop.

Developing a supportive relationship is not something which can be described in general terms; each relationship is unique and requires an idiosyncratic approach. Nevertheless, trust has to be at the core, and underpinning this is a need to provide support which is reliable and consistent. The young people we are talking about sometimes almost entirely lack a sense of safety, and need people around them who can in some small measure provide a solid and predictable measure of strength, a cement which can piece together fragments of trust. Under these circumstances, there is a clear need for supportive relationships provided by professionals which can supplement existing close relationships (Spratt *et al.* 2010). There is a possibility that, if this is the case, problems will be prevented from escalating. Young people have indicated that relationships with professionals need to be based on respect for the young person, continuity and trustworthiness (Philip and Spratt 2010). As the three elements are sought after and developed amongst professionals, the hallmark of this work, that of responding to young people's professed wishes, will inform the help offered and lead to positive outcomes.

CHAPTER 6

Visions of Spirituality

At this point, I feel I should convey to the reader my hope that each of us will have acquired more than a superficial understanding of the stories of Terry, Scott, Rose, Karl and Coral. More importantly, that this deeper view may have been encouraged in some measure to be applied to the ways we respond to other young people who have suffered trauma and abuse.

However, there is one aspect of their 'being' which I feel impressed to focus on. This aspect sprouts from and revolves around all that has gone before. The reason I raise this as a possibility is that each theme of their lives, their stories, their voices, their emotionality, their coping strategies and their relationships do not seem to encompass the whole individual. Unquestionably there have been some repetitions, as these themes have overlapped, possessed congruity and have sometimes fluidly replaced or displaced one another. In contrast to this, there has remained a feeling of holes or gaps in the fabric which has been woven. Whereas some areas have been thick with interwoven themes, others have appeared to lack clear definition and have remained strangely void of any identity. This led me to believe that I was missing something of a profound nature which might just find its place in the patches of seemingly thin fabric.

There were some particular expressions, some specific deeper voiced concerns and ideas which drew my attention with such force that they came into my mind repeatedly, and would not go away. These were expressions, apparently deep-felt and personal, which appear to emanate from somewhere else. A new theme was badgering me and it possessed a profound individuality, which I believe, every one of us possesses.

Each young person revealed a capacity to interpret their lives in ways beyond that which would have been expected from their experience. My mind was caught by the hopefulness of their voices at first, but this grew into the recognition of a deeper attribute, which was based on heart-felt emotions and deeply held beliefs.

The idea, that each young person was creative in forming a vision for their lives, crept up on me during the time when I thought I had come to the end of thinking deeply about their stories. The theme of a personal vision had materialised, representing that which encompasses the evidence of what I feel can be defined as the spirituality of each young person. Spirituality is used here as a means of expressing those aspects of the young people's stories which simply express a desire to look beyond themselves and their material lives. Relationships with others appear significant here also, and so these are included in particular ways within each personal vision. Similarly, their visions possess elements of personal identity which are to do with a sense of worth and harmony, which appear to be bound up with spirituality.

The complexity of this idea mirrors the complexity of the young people's lives, where 'waves of resiliency' are present but seem to be dependent on the spirituality and emotionality of the young person, along with the specificity of their relationships and experiences. These all appeared to contribute to the complexity and intimate nature of each young person's identity.

The spirituality of each young person resonates with certain common characteristics which have been used to define this attribute as 'a desire to look beyond themselves and their material world' (Collis 2009, p.348). However, the idiosyncratic qualities associated with spirituality such as variations in tendency, expression and practice need to be considered. Spirituality varies 'in terms of context, frequency, intensity, and so on, often having the character of gentle intimations of a guiding or loving presence, a sense of harmony or wellbeing, a feeling of burdens or pain being lifted, or awareness of a life force running through all things' (Woods and Woods 2008, p.103).

The definition which will guide these comments is based on a holistic view and which describes spirituality as 'a way to reach beyond ourselves and our existing knowledge to search for explanations of existence' (Stolberg 2008, p.171). The search leads to an 'ethical elevation, a sense of reinforcement of an orientation to the moral purpose of change and to the raising of aspirations to a higher goal' (Woods and Woods 2008, p.104). 'People are being helped to move on' and 'answers and inspiration' are received (ibid., p.109). These are the kinds of expressions which young people may use to try and describe spiritual influences in their lives.

It is this day-to-day aspect of spirituality which the young people speak of as they recognise influences which have brought them to places where ethical questions are answered and change and commitment to causes other than their own occur. Rose gave voice to a desire for a moral rightness in her life.

So I tried to do everything I could so that my mum wouldn't get beaten up... So it was a case of doing the right thing at that point.

I did like PE when I was little because it was active and it was just like... Oh, a breath of fresh air really...

When I was young, I used to think to myself this isn't going to be for ever...

I'm trying to make up for it now...'cos like I try to be there for her (sister)... I'm really nice to her now...

Rose's story reveals a tender desire to reinstate justice in her life. Her connection to herself and others is based on the rightness or otherwise of her feelings and thoughts. The joy she felt in the 'fresh air' is echoed by her longing to do 'the right thing' and her clinging to the hope of better things to come. She urges herself to go higher without consciously knowing where the energy, motivation or inspiration is coming from. She recognises her auntie as being in some way responsible for triggering her aspirations, but maintains them despite her emotional voice which speaks of her prolonged suffering.

Others fuel her spirit with encouragement: 'I've been able to be myself...since — (support worker) worked with me it has been a lot easier. I've actually become myself...really.' The 'picture' she has of herself has become brighter and more vivid. She has obtained a clearer vision of her own capabilities, her own shortcomings and her ability to change. She recognises the truth of her mother 'having put her through a lot' and is able to smile and say, 'I feel it's ok for me to do my own thing now and my mum hasn't got to be there all the time.' Rose is expressing a profound sense of being free, not just of the pain which caused her to self-harm, but of those bonds which could have tied her down.

Rose is looking beyond her world and the ties of the past, and her story powerfully reflects the excitement of a journey forward and upward to a greater hope and peace:

You can do whatever you want...

Coral's quiet and reflective ways almost conceal her longing for change and improvement. Her vision of a better life has at its root an understanding of the part she needed to play in bringing it about. This knowledge emerged from an analysis based on observation and on powerful feelings which she was not afraid to act upon. Boler raises this as being something that needs to be taught 'to define and identify how and when particular emotions inform and define knowledge' (1999, p.142). Coral's use of her agency was to make things better for others and, directly or indirectly, for herself. Her unselfish vision had inspired her to 'tell her mum' and then to follow through by trying to avoid any upset for her mum, so that there was little chance of her going back to her dad. Her plan and the execution of it proved to be completely achievable.

Throughout, she had appeared to travel alone, except for the burden of advising her mum and supporting her brothers. Her happiness lay in the achievement of something out of 'nothing'. Her inner fortitude and her desire to achieve a better life committed her to a particular path which was created by her and which had in fact brought happiness. The power which emanates from Coral's vision has grown from her awareness of her own possibilities, combined with a realisation that her feelings had provided her with a sense of direction and purpose. The 'numbness' which some speak of after experiencing abuse is not present. Feelings of hopefulness and assurance have spurred Coral on to do all she can to change her family's experiences of abuse.

Scott has also indicated within his story that recognition of the alignment of powerful feelings with specific experiences had led him to evaluate what was happening and adopt a new vision of himself which had found fulfilment in some profound changes:

I think I cope just by staking in there basically, having faith and stuff because I am a Christian. So I pray and stuff like that and things.

...they pray and stuff...talk to me about things.

I actually wanted to...help people who have had experiences and stuff and use my experiences and...basically knowledge and everything to help other people...I've been asking around for that.

His vision drew on many attributes. His own 'silliness' was at the forefront. His thinking was extensive and prolonged. He recognised that what he had become was not how he wanted to be and ethical questions had had to be confronted and answered. Finally his aggressive attitudes were redirected into an active and assertive belief that he was able to 'help other people'. He was then ready to consult and 'check out' (Boler 1999) the consequences of the decision he had made which was to 'change'.

The story contains a myriad of dimensions which point to 'waves of resilience' from a multitude of sources. Scott's reflective and meditative practices which come readily to him seem to play a part. His affirmative responses to the church members, the social workers and one particular teacher whom he had known for four years relay a readiness to be accepting of others and a willingness to communicate. There were 'too many to remember basically…lots' who had at one time or another spent time with him. They seem to have communicated attributes and skills which he was drawn to, and which provided him with a vision of what he wanted to become. He hadn't been talking to his family, but there were others, who possessed qualities which he favoured and wanted to replicate, who made themselves available to him.

It seems likely that a large proportion of his vision for himself and for his life came from them. However, Scott's introspective actions were self-induced. He saw beyond the boundaries of the police cell in which he found himself, and far from undermining and desensitising him it proved to be the catalyst for the production of powerful emotions which would encourage him to look beyond his experiences, to see things differently and change. The outward sign of his looking beyond his experiences of abuse was the diffusion of the disempowering emotion of aggression and his move towards compassion and peacefulness. This move was created by Scott, but he was assisted by several caring professionals who provided the emotional support he needed.

Seeing things differently, forming a change of vision, is a theme which is to be found in differing situations in Terry's story.

Terry is ready to challenge his own perceptions and assumptions because of his willingness to see things differently. The most obvious example of this is the change he creates in his relationship with his sister's boyfriend. He is 'cool', possessing those qualities which Terry wants to be associated with, to be in a 'gang' together. A way of seeing through and beyond the colour of someone's skin and all the associations built up over time which would have prevented an open and trusting relationship has been achieved by Terry. There is not a vestige of prejudice or uncertainty remaining.

Seeing his father differently is a strong theme within Terry's story. He had been helpless in preventing injury to his mother, and had 'cried' because he told himself 'I could have stopped that but I didn't.' He had further known that his father would have injured him if he had intervened:

I knew he would have gone for me.

A dramatic change has occurred in how Terry deals with his father that demonstrates a complete diversion away from desperate tears to a new-found vision of his father who can be challenged, and who is no longer threatening or disempowering. He is even able to encourage his mother in thinking and seeing his dad differently and congratulates her on what he sees as her change to seeing him as he really is, a person who wanted to control her.

There is a change too in his mother's attitude to her brother, who she had in the past dismissed as being 'a bit stupid'. Terry 'always liked him' and had held strongly to his feelings despite both his mother and father disagreeing. Terry saw that his mother had 'changed' her feelings towards her brother, and that his influence was felt more; she had recognised that her attitudes had been controlled by Terry's dad. Now Terry and his mum had something of a shared vision of their past and they were able to conform and agree more easily with one another.

The clarity of Terry's vision of what had happened to him and his mum is obvious, and is particularly evident when he states that his dad is really the one who should be going to the 'psycho' hospital. His sense of what is right informed him of the kind of justice which should be meted out, and then he had come to a possible solution. Terry never accepted the abuse because he has within him a profound moral sense which governs his choices and his attitudes.

This sense is crucial and acts as a very effective 'wave of resilience' for him as it provides him with the means of discrediting the harmful and disrespectful actions of others. He gazes out at unfairness and injustice and recognises it. This allows him to disqualify it, and consign it to a place where it no longer hurts. His suffering voice can still be felt but it is tempered by compassion and the beginnings of an inner peace which is founded on his clear understanding of what is right and wrong:

He (dad) pretended he didn't know her (sister)...if I told her she really wouldn't like it...and she would cry and I don't want to see her cry, 'cos we've all cried enough.

Karl's vision of change rests on his willingness to be flexible in times of great uncertainty. His openness to the unexpected is heart-warming and surprising.

Karl accepts the changes in his life and sees them as opportunities. His expectations are not really formed, and so it seems to be comparatively easy for him to embrace whatever comes his way. This is not due to indifference but a form of contentment with his life, which can only be threatened by others who let him down. His vision of his own existence is therefore dependent upon how he deals with those who prove untrustworthy, and in particular his father. Because Karl's willingness to accept what happens is so strong, it is only left to him to deal with the consequences of his father's behaviour. His sky is relatively unclouded, except for one very dark cloud, which demands his attention. He copes by 'ignoring' and confining it to a place where it will have no impact upon him. So, his world returns to being sunny and bright. Karl is clearly an optimistic young man who will probably find peace and contentment wherever he goes. His emotionality and spirituality are wrapped up in his new family circumstances which have gradually dispelled his anxious concerns about his father one day finding them. Of all the young people, he stands out as the one who possessed a 'wave of resilience' which required little or no assistance to work. It appears to be intrinsic to him, and has powerfully sustained him through loss, hardship and uncertainty.

Each of the young people discussed here appeared to grasp and apply a vision of their situation which encompassed desires, qualities and expectations which intrinsically were able to build a positive outlook, and have a desired effect on their thinking and behaviour. As I thought about each of the young people, it was their hopefulness which had in the first instance triggered my attention. The obvious question which needs to be asked is, 'In so much darkness, where does the light of hope spring from?' Young people's lives are indeed dark as they journey through experiences of domestic violence, and yet despair gives way, and hopeful visions enter. What happens for such a change to take place?

Encouragement of positive thinking has been a popular ploy to bring about an improvement in people's mental health and emotional wellbeing. This has been affected by encouraging each child and young person to know that they are not the cause of the abuse. Understandably, guilt and self-blame would interfere with positive feelings towards themselves, and might destroy all vestiges of a positive self-image. Similarly, to lead a child or young person to a place where they would have no difficulty in feeling better about themselves is a strategy which is sometimes employed. Some projects aim to provide them with opportunities to learn new skills, to discover aptitudes and talents, and to have fun with others who also need to feel better about themselves. Support of this kind has proved to have its value, providing a more positive framework in which the child or young person has every encouragement to see themselves in a more positive light.

Therapeutic interventions through mental health agencies have sometimes provided children and young people with much-needed answers. Positive attitudes can generally only prevail when worries, caused by experiences which make no sense and which pose many unanswered questions, are voiced and reflected upon. The appropriate forum for this to happen safely may be sessions with a qualified therapist or counsellor. Judgements in relation to this kind of intervention would need to be considered very carefully. I stress this because one unsatisfactory experience for a child, when worries are not dissipated, may well have long-term effects, in that the young person may have a negative view of therapy, and reject further offers when it is clear there is a need.

However, therapeutic work can sometimes provide much-needed answers, and can lead a child or young person to recognise and know their own worth, together with a strong realisation of their identity. Many young people may depend on an acknowledgement of their faith and beliefs as part of this process. Just as I have advocated the importance of giving children and young people permission to share their stories, their emotions, their ways of coping and their views of people, I would stress the crucial nature of allowing them to share their deepest perceptions of the meanings of their own lives, and what they see as the purpose of their existence.

Children and young people need to be encouraged to explore their own lives, and as they respond, they will find fulfilment in meeting a need which I have found they all appear to possess, which is an insatiable appetite to learn, to grow and to make sense of their lives, and to consider who they are. The vision they possess may be immeasurably valuable to them because it may provide them with a powerful resource in overcoming painful and insecure feelings. As supportive adults there needs to be an awareness of the potential of this source of healing, that we may be able to assist young people in becoming aware of their own spirituality.

CHAPTER 7

Helping into Wholeness

The multiple strands of young people's stories lead to the belief that there needs to be an effort to understand those aspects of development which might encompass multiple strands and achieve a sense of 'wholeness'. Unpicking lives, as has been done here, and isolating themes, inevitably leads to a pile of unpicked material, which, hopefully has its benefits, but which needs to find a constructed form which is characterised by the welding together and amalgamation of its separate components. Viewing complexity and appreciating variableness has to be viewed with a desire to integrate and at some point see the person as knit together and 'whole' once again.

The idea of support into wholeness is considered here. Support is defined as specific provisions and help which young people may receive, some of which have been described in the stories told. These provisions can be acquired and understood by a supporter or provider through training, or they may be inbuilt and based on a natural ability and desire to be supportive. However, they are all dependent upon a built foundation which enables the young person to reflect upon her/his experiences without fear or possibility of rejection.

'Wholeness'

At this point, it is my aim to broaden the discussion further by introducing the idea of 'wholeness' as being a credible and desirable attribute for all. In this way, the context of this work is being shaped into something much more general. The lives of the five young people deserve to be placed with others, that there might be an evaluation of their suffering and healing in relation to the experiences of others who have also suffered and who need to heal into wholeness.

It has appeared that a very significant influence on the young people's ability to form or impose 'waves of resilience' is their sense of identity, which I will liken to their sense of 'wholeness' (Zappone 1991). This would be an enfolding of their creativity, their emotionality, their physicality, including their sense of security and safety, their sociality, their spirituality and their thinking (this is not expressed in an order of importance). Sometimes, it may be that we are at fault because we overlook the complexity of wholeness and disregard the whole 'picture'. We may neglect to see how each aspect plays an essential part in the whole wellbeing of children and young people.

Each of us, I would like to believe, needs to feel and be 'whole'. The feeling of wholeness seems to be grounded in an inner integrity which emanates from the acceptance of consistent actions and thoughts which are habitually relied upon to bring comfort and satisfaction. Coral worked hard at school, and withdrew to her bedroom. Terry defended his mum and defied his dad. Scott listened to professionals and learned from them, applying what he learnt to his own life and the lives of others. Rose became independent and developed intimate friendships. Karl played with other children, and recollected the domestic violence in relatively innocuous terms.

Each of the young people discovered what worked for them, and formed habits in their lives which underpinned their coping capabilities. Helping young people form habitual behaviours which are self-enhancing and productive appears to be crucial.

Understanding how these habits are formed is critical to understanding wholeness. Every person establishes patterns of behaviour, but clearly these patterns will be influenced by suffering and disempowering emotions such as fearfulness, aggressiveness and bitterness. Rose went through a 'phase' of self-harm. Scott went through a 'phase' of abusing his mum. Coral went through a 'phase' of self-induced isolation and friendlessness. These behaviours are described as 'phases' because they proved to be transitory in the young people's stories. Nevertheless, the behaviours were well established, if only for a relatively short period of time, but seemingly did not result in long-term emotional, spiritual, mental or social damage.

The apparent lack of long-term damage seems to be due to each person's sense of personal integrity and positive self-image which was in some measure built up by the supportive provisions supplied by friends, family and professionals. This is why these provisions are crucial, allowing the young people the potential to throw out destructive 'phases' and construct behaviours which will add to their feelings of wholeness.

Further studies, focusing on this idea of wholeness in relation to supporting children who have suffered domestic violence and abuse, would be welcome. However, there is some evidence here to support the idea that wholeness is a critical factor. Where there is present the recognition of its centrality to healing, a young person is likely to benefit. It is significant that the negative patterns of behaviour and thinking were arrested or modified in some measure because of steady, appropriate, reliable and empowering help, which focused holistically on each young person's inner integrity and self-worth. Underpinning these provisions of support is each young person's view of themselves, and this has to be at the foundation of all supportive measures.

Provisions of support are now described in relation to the research undertaken by myself and others. This conclusion is based on evidence, theory, experience and some subjective views based on experience, and is constructed with the hope that it will instigate debate and inspire reflection amongst professional practitioners. The object is to encourage ideas and practices which place children and young people at the centre, and provide a much-needed consideration to the concept of supporting them into wholeness.

Provision: helping to see the self as ok

Coral had declared that she wanted to tell her story because she hoped that her experiences could help others. Her voice has taught me that I needed her story, and the stories of other children and young people, and it has helped me in such a way that I was able to piece together some of my own fragmented perceptions of the effects of domestic violence on young people.

This has led me to feel more confident in assessing how best I might be supportive to other children and young people, and how I might be able to offer advice to others. It has also led me to understand my own story a little more clearly, as I have inevitably struggled with the disempowering and traumatising consequences of abusive relationships. It has led me to be helped, and to see myself as ok. My hope is that readers of this will find similar rewards, in that they will see children and young people differently, and want to support them into wholeness.

The idea that the young people have thoughts which show clarity of understanding and a sureness of the part they are able to play as experiences unfold is accepted here. It must be recorded that receiving help and professional support from a worker trained in domestic violence may well be a prerequisite for this to happen. For each child the understanding of personal experience is unique, but for some it would seem the specialist help may well be crucial in the development of a positive identity.

Asked how he had got stronger, after receiving support from several workers, Scott replied:

> I think it was…experiences, witnessing things and just the knowledge and everything.

The stories of the young people display the importance of giving them 'permission' to explore their experiences, facilitating the growth of knowledge and understanding of their histories (Park 1999).

This clearly demonstrates the critical part played by the opportunities provided to all young people for them to explore their experiences, for them to be listened to, to encourage their deepening awareness that there exist those who can support them, and who accept and respect them as they are. The space they are given may provide each young person the means to 'wash away' those attitudes, feelings and thoughts which had silenced them. As they come to 'know' their stories and to articulate their pain, and reflect on those experiences which had caused them suffering and isolation, each young person may gain the power to understand themselves and their experiences with greater clarity. Each may find ways to move from disempowering to humanising emotions, to travel towards being able to feel hope, compassion and peacefulness.

The space offered to young people to examine and reflect on their lives may enable them to form 'waves of resilience'. In the case of Coral, it has been noted earlier that she had remained alone during the violence. She spoke to no one except her mother, and she coped by getting on with her work at school, not having any friends and going to her room when she felt she needed to. The space she needed she had created herself, and she remained dependent on herself for any 'waves of resilience' which would sustain her. On the surface, Coral appears to be a young person who had suffered less from the effects of domestic violence, but the analysis shows that she was thrown back on her own inner resources, which proved to sustain her, but which were stretched to their limits.

The 'waves' she created as she remained in solitude held her suffering in check, but she admits that later she recognised the need for her to enter another kind of space where she was allowed and enabled to make sense of her life; and then, only then, was she in a position to 'help others'. Every young person deserves this kind of opportunity. Every child and young person can achieve a sense of being ok, a sense of wholeness.

Provision: helping to recognise the uniqueness of each voice

Every story has the potential to produce a myriad of interpretations, which may develop to a point where it is far from easy to draw neat, succinct conclusions and make unambiguous inferences. It has become evident that every young person has a particular and unique voice which describes the complexity of each of their individual lives. The deserving recognition of each of their personal, distinct and special stories is stressed here as valuable, critical and beneficial.

Each young person has revealed her or his story so that interpretive analysis was possible. Layer upon layer of interpretations has brought forth a deeper understanding of each of the young people and an appreciation of their particular 'waves of resilience'. In essence their voices need to be remembered as expressions of their unique identity. Individual work is appropriately designed for this. 'One-to-one work can meet children's needs, particularly around adjustment, emotions and behaviour' (Mullender 2005, p.5).

The voices of children and young people represent and encompass each young person's identity, sense of autonomy and personal rights, independence, empowerment and emotional journey. As a voice is listened to, it provides a way of looking at the standing and strengths of the young person as the story is told. It encompasses those aspects of young people's lives which express how they see themselves and what makes them unique and independent of others. It also points to those 'waves of resilience' which are self-induced, self-motivated and which appear to be independent of the influence of others.

The expression of self and identity is evidence that every young person possesses a degree of self-awareness, belief and knowledge which may support her or him through times of adversity. It is suggested that efforts to deepen the self-understanding of a young person will enhance her or his ability to cope with challenges. One way this might be achieved is based on the pivotal premise of this book which was to offer young people opportunities to reflect upon and give voice to their experiences. Something entirely unique occurs when we raise our thoughts from inner worlds into outward expressions. It would appear that making sense of experience requires reflection and expression, and with the making sense, further inroads are made into self-knowledge and an understanding of influences which have moulded our character and our thinking.

Provision of recognition: helping to see

We have learnt that Coral had remained with her thoughts in isolation while the domestic violence had continued. At the time of her being offered support, she had spoken only to her mother, and of necessity had excluded expressing those thoughts which she saw as potentially damaging to her relationship with her mother. However, when the time came, she responded positively to the opportunity offered to her to share her inner thoughts and perceptions of what had occurred. She gained revelatory insights into her relationship with her dad, and about other men. She began to recognise the strengths and weaknesses of other relationships, and, fundamentally, she began to see herself in a much more positive way. This was achieved through another's recognition of her as an individual whose life had been filled with suffering; but yet, importantly, that individual was strong enough to listen to her pain, could stay with her and acknowledge that the suffering was not in vain, and that it should not be ignored or forgotten. As part of a life, it had value and meaning, and in no way detracted from the wonder and significance of that life.

As a young person is supported to value their life and appreciate their individual worth, a transforming influence comes into their life which has the potential to dispel the anxieties and worthless feelings which are associated with past suffering. A life which is valued provides the foundation for an unimpaired verbalisation of experience. With this flow of communication comes a deepening awareness of the self and an understanding that all experience can be empowering and safely talked about without fear of rejection or personal damage. Helping a young person see themselves and others with greater clarity through encouraging ways of building trust with others and self-belief may result in an increase in empowerment and emotional stability.

Provision: helping to encourage mastery

'Helplessness' is seen as a product of disempowerment and suffering where there has been a lack of opportunity to 'open up experiences' (Park 1999) and there has been an erosion of the young person's basic rights. Seligman describes the change from helplessness to mastery as a demonstration of a young person's knowledge of himself, 'to know himself, to be curious about his theory of himself and of the world... to take an active stance in his world, and to shape his own life, rather than be a passive recipient of what happens his way. He is equipped to persevere in the face of adversity and to struggle to overcome his problems' (2007, p.297).

Looking for and encouraging self-knowledge appears to be fundamental to change. Self-knowledge brings the possibility of change, of growth and the use of a wide range of abilities and skills which when recognised and appreciated can be applied and used, making management of situations and emotions possible:

I picked up lots of skills what people do.

I stayed out of the way for quite a while...wanted to be my own person. I need time to act like a child.

I was keeping a lot of stuff inside...now that it's all out and I've told — everything, I feel that it's always going to be there but I can kind of move on.

Young people may display a surety emerging from their sense of identity which may prevail and surmount the uncertainty of their lives. They are not passive bystanders, but active participants (Mullender *et al.* 2002):

I would have a sort of weird feeling that I knew there would be an argument.

It just made everything worse...so I stopped joining in with her (mum).

Well, I was the one actually who told my mum that we had to get away and tried to make her do it.

She'll (mum) be safe 'cos I know I can defend her.

I knew exactly what to do…just smile and give her (mum) a hug and anything like that.

It's quite a release…a relief to know that she (mum) put us through quite a bit, but in the same way, I do think, yeh, you did…

As we seek to provide young people with opportunities for self-expression, we also need to encourage autonomy, giving them a sense of their being masters of their own course. As a prerequisite to effective support, we must consider that we may need to stand back and provide them with opportunities to grow in confidence by making decisions and encouraging them to act upon them.

Provision: helping to inspire hope

Hopefulness was evident very early on as I reflected on the young people's stories. Rose's 'picture' of the time when things would be better remained a very powerful image. Scott's desire to 'change' and his ability to put his desire into action was based on the hope that he could be better than he had been. Coral's sudden realisation that not all men in her life were like her father, and that there was the definite possibility that someday, somehow, she could have a positive relationship with a man, shows that her hopefulness was in some way ignited. Terry's hope was centred upon the time when all the pain would be gone, and which had been drawn from the words of a trusted member of his family. Karl possessed a hopefulness which put paid to the losses in his life, and moved him into a world where pain evaporated in a self-induced mist of distractions. Rose possessed hope for herself, that she would ultimately be able to change the suffering of her life into a healthy life. This is generally true of all the young people. They had reason to believe in a better future.

It is important to realise at this point that instilling hope, or inspiring hope, is a critical part of effective help. The belief that debilitating and destructive experience need not have a never-ending negative impact on a life needs to be held and acted upon by those who provide support. The value of the experience must be expressed, which may open up the possibility of utilising the experiences gained in positive ways. Scott used his experience and 'knowledge' to provide supportive care to his friends and peers. Coral saw the potential of being able to 'help' others because of her experiences. To use every kind of experience in this way exhibits a hopefulness beyond what would be expected. Each young person may be willing to be a provider, because they see their future in terms of creating something out of their experience which may be wholly beneficial.

The hopefulness which may be generated out of dire and destructive experiences seems to come about through what may be described as targeted encouragement, which appeals to an aspect of the young person which the support worker may recognise as being very influential. The words and interactions which inspire young people need to be clearly encouraging. They may encourage beliefs that things can change, that people can be kind, that each of us can make a difference in a good way. Encouraging language is remembered and used to comfort and to motivate. It adds an element of brightness to a dark and otherwise depressing life, which helps the young person to hold on, and lightens their burdens and lessens their pain.

Encouragement designed with an understanding of the child or young person in mind may have short-term and long-term benefits in alleviating distress and offering hope, and the possibility of some healing into wholeness.

Provision: conditions which help create 'waves of resilience'

Scott, a young man troubled by aggressive feelings, has become someone capable of the most caring compassion, and intrinsic desire to help others. Ultimately, his acceptance of the help that was offered to him, and his desire to 'change', had taken him to a place of peace, despite his continuing struggles at school. Scott's waves of resilience were formed by a spiritual connection with what had given him 'good' feelings, and with those trusted others who had remained with him consistently on his journey through suffering. It seems that of all the young people, his coping was dependent upon a mix of these 'waves', and demonstrates how an individual fuses internal and external elements of their lives to move forward confidently and happily. Scott needed intensive support over a protracted period of time for these 'waves' to become evident.

Some young people have inner waves, I am sure, which require just the right conditions for them to take effect. In Scott's life, the right conditions appear to have been many people providing these conditions. There were many who gave their time, their interest, their care to Scott.

Included in these was Scott's family. Everyone persevered with him, despite his apparent disdain of them. It took a while for 'the penny to drop'. Inevitably, however, it did, because the conditions for the change had been created by many people who had not given up on him. Some young people will need a range of provisions, over a protracted period, which are repeated before they can make decisive changes.

Coral, perhaps the most independent of all the young people, showed how important the relationship between a mother and child can be. The most significant 'wave of resilience' lay in her belief that her mother was implicitly alright, and would choose to do what needed to be done to protect herself and her children, once she had been given permission to do so. Coral's role in the giving of permission was remarkable, and it is this that underpins the happy outcome of her family's story. Her tenacity, emotional regulation and self-reliance provided her with the resources to lead her family, without any visible external support. Coral's 'voice' penetrates the suffering, and calmly resonates a peaceful and contented present. The conditions for Coral were created by her mother and one support worker. That was all that was required, and the time was relatively short. The timing had been crucial. Her mum had first taken the step to accept support, and once that had been achieved, and she had become more stable, Coral was able to feel secure enough to accept that she too would need to talk about her experiences.

As we consider supporting young people who have become isolated, we will need to be sensitive and careful in the way support is given. We will need to be aware of those internal strengths which have maintained a young person through times of aloneness and suffering.

Terry shares his troubled view of the world, but shows that he, too, has a desire to share the precious fragments of light which have pierced the terrible darkness of his past. Of all the young people, Terry's story of suffering is fresher and less diffused than the others. The reasons for this are unclear, but his 'view' of the significant people in his life is strong, vivid and powerful. Terry needs to be clear about who he can trust, and it is through his own understanding of his relationships that he has been able to develop 'waves of resilience', and find happiness within his family. For Terry, the conditions for the creation of his waves of resilience lie in those relationships which have been completely reliable and unshakeable. In this way, his family has played a significant role in forming the right conditions.

As we support young people who appear to have a network of family and others around them, we will need to see how this network might be strengthened and applied more effectively through discovering the views of the young person. As a comprehensive picture of their networks emerges, it will be necessary to implant in the young people's minds the value of those who are naturally in their lives. Remember, a support worker will inevitably leave.

Karl's inner desire and ability to remove the damaging experiences of his past from his mind and his heart have enabled him to cope with extreme loss, and accept the past without recrimination. His story reveals a remarkable inner fortitude, and a calm assurance that everything would work out for the best. His faith in those around him, and his hopeful optimism that life would get better, are hallmarks of his story. Karl is measured in the telling of his story, echoing the way he was able to express his emotionality. Emotional regulation and hopefulness appear to wash away his feelings of loss, and his 'voice' remains constant and positive. The conditions for Karl were largely created by himself. This is surprising but not unlikely, as we must remember that not all young people need support, and some cope without it apparently.

Consideration must be given to the possibility that a young person is ok. The role of the support worker may be simply to put across those fundamental truths which need to be fully understood by all children. These would include that all violence is wrong, that the perpetrator alone is responsible for the abuse, and if the young person is availed of group work that 'they are not the only one who has lived with violence' (Mullender 2005).

Rose has told her story in a way which emphasises her emotional, social, spiritual and intellectual journey. Of all the young people, Rose's voice, views of relationships and vision are pieces of her story which share equal power. It was her hopeful voice that first caught my attention. Later, I became aware of her emotional journey towards healing. Finally, I recognised that Rose's story was the one most closely aligned to my own, and this has led me to a deep appreciation of what she had achieved at such a tender age. The coping pathways that she had followed were bound up with her mother, and with self-expression and identity. I have come to realise that this has clear parallels with my own story.

As I reflected on my interpretation of Rose's story, I am reminded of my deep involvement in their stories. Rose has journeyed most significantly, and has reached a place where happier relationships and hoped-for visions are being accomplished. The conditions for her had been created by a support worker who provided her with a belief in herself, and an aunt who had given her hope. This, combined with a clear understanding of the moral dimension of life, had led Rose to appreciate her place and her contribution in caring for others.

Identifying a young person's waves of resilience is a useful exercise in finding what works for an individual, and then being able to work with what works. For example, a young person who enjoys self-expression may be offered opportunities to do just that in a variety of ways, for example sport, art, creative writing or music. This may form a significant 'wave' and contribute greatly to the young person's feelings of positive self-worth and wholeness. The thoughts and ideas offered here are only a few. As we become more adept at recognising a young person's 'waves of resilience', we will be able to fashion appropriate support accordingly.

Young people and us

Young people's suffering does not have to stand in the way of their being able to act courageously and selflessly. Their voices are now in the public domain and this has fuelled my determination to work with an increased effort to empower young victims of domestic violence and facilitate their wishes. Their remarkable bravery and sureness about what they see as the correct course has taught me about their undoubted strengths and struggles.

Young people are certainly imbued with many 'waves of resilience' which are inspired by a complex interplay of intrinsic and extrinsic factors. Each young person's experiences are unique, but they do reveal the crucial nature of a distinctive package of support, the efficacy of which seems to depend almost entirely upon the establishment of personal relationships between the young person and those who are available, insightful, sensitive and willing.

Stories of the young people underline the need for specific support for victims of domestic violence. The availability of the kind of support which the young people valued and described as being beneficial will need to be considered in relation to the family, friends and others who may be in a position to offer it. This in turn promotes the idea of a deeper understanding of the effects of domestic violence amongst professionals, so support can become all-embracing. Training specifically designed to raise awareness of the effects of domestic violence on children and young people, together with opportunities to reflect upon the kind of support which professionals can offer, needs to be available. Voluntary agencies which specialise in domestic violence and abuse such as Women's Aid, the Hampton Trust and many others have the potential to offer professional training, but sometimes lack the means to do so.

Young people needed arms around them to comfort them and uphold them at various times in their stories. I hope that all children and young people exposed to domestic violence will have access to the kind of comfort and help appropriate to them, and will be able to access the kinds of provision described here.

Effective support may guide a child or young person from a position where disempowering emotions hold precedence, or were highly influential, to a place where humanising emotions hold them on a course which empowers them into self-belief and hopeful aspirations. The emotional journeys of every young person need to be traced through their suffering voices to the emergence of their healing voices. The nature of young people's voices needs to be understood, and help needs to be sensitive to where they are on their emotional journey.

Awareness of the complexity, uniqueness and convergence of emotions has been raised and with it a clear need to further explore emotional journeys and support, and how emotional wellbeing can be fostered within the context of social, historical and gender issues surrounding domestic violence. Young people's stories may clearly define the impact on their emotional wellbeing in an uncompromising way. At times of acute distress, they may need unequivocal messages which are utterly consistent with a respect for their voice and identity, their view of their relationships and their vision of what could be achieved despite their pain.

The implications of young people's stories are that there needs to be a joined-up approach encapsulating three elements: first, their views of significant relationships; second, their visions of spiritual facets of their lives; and third, their unique voices in relation to their stories. Each young person needs to be sustained and encouraged to find those sources of resilience and support which contribute to her or his emotional and spiritual wellbeing or 'wholeness'.

The voices of young people are clear and unequivocal. Despite the complexity of experience, clarity is the hallmark of what they have to say. So much of what they talk about is unambiguous, and reflects a desire to be understood. Those things which occur to prevent young people talking about their suffering need to be dismissed. Their main motivation appears to be based on deeply held desires and feelings which seem to be to help others, and this may well guide their words and actions.

My own journey through suffering has been marked by some significant changes as my life has been touched by many young people. My work has become more focused on the needs of children and young people who have witnessed or experienced abuse, as I have recognised that I might be able to offer an effective support to them or be able to ascertain or encourage appropriate support wherever it might be found. Just as the young people began to hope for something better for themselves and those around them, my hopes and wishes have evolved into feeling very much the same.

The safety of young people will always be the first priority. The safety and wellbeing of children and young people as a whole, and in particular those who have experienced domestic violence and abuse, has become the focus of my working life. I continue to be aware of the prevalence of domestic violence within families, and continue to work with children and young people who live with it.

To conclude, the voices of children and young people are not universally recognised. This book supports the need for a vigorous effort to rectify this error. The intention here is to raise an indisputable actuality that there is a need to accept that children and young people have a crucial amount to give and must be provided with opportunities to make a contribution to policy and professional practice. By so doing, their understandings of their experience could underpin decisions and actions which directly affect them.

The power of the personal testimonies of five young people cannot be denied. I hope that their extraordinary stories and others like them will be recognised, valued and acted upon so that all may learn and benefit from them. As each child and young person enters our world, and we more importantly enter theirs, may we be mindful of the need to place them at the heart of our endeavours, and seek to support and empower them, supplying a provision which helps in the development of each child's sense of their own 'wholeness'.

References

Ackermann, D. (1996) 'The Alchemy of Risk, Struggle, and Hope.' In M. Mananzan *et al.* (eds) *Women Resisting Violence.* New York: Orbis.

Alldred, P. (1998) 'Ethnography and Discourse Analysis: Dilemmas in Representing the Voices of Children.' In J. Ribbens and R. Edwards (eds) *Feminist Dilemmas in Qualitative Research.* London: Sage.

Aviles, A., Anderson, T. and Davila, E. (2006) 'Socio-emotional development within the context of the school.' *Child and Adolescent Mental Health 11,* 1, 32–39.

Bell, J. and Stanley, N. (2006) 'Learning about domestic violence: young people's responses to a Healthy Relationships programme.' *Sex Education 6,* 3, 237–250.

Bellhouse, B., Fuller, A. and Johnson G. (2005) *Managing the Difficult Emotions.* London: Sage.

Bellous, J. (2008) Editorial. *International Journal of Children's Spirituality 13,* 3, 195–201.

Berlant, L. (ed.) (2004) *Compassion.* London: Routledge.

Boler, M. (1999) *Feeling Power.* New York: Routledge.

Bolton, G. (2005) *Reflective Practice.* London: Sage.

Bone, J. (2008) 'Exploring trauma, loss and healing: spirituality, Te Whariki and early childhood education.' *International Journal of Children's Spirituality 13,* 3, 265–276.

Bowlby, J. (1981) *Attachment and Loss.* London: Penguin.

Bowlby, J. (1988) *A Secure Base.* London: Routledge.

Brueggemann, W. (2000) *Deep Memory, Exuberant Hope.* Minneapolis: Fortress Press.

Burstow, B. (1992) *Radical Feminist Therapy.* Newbury Park, CA: Sage.

CAMHS (2008) *Children and Young People in Mind.* Available at www.dh.gov.uk/en/ Publicationsandstatistics/Publications/PublicationsPolicyAndGuidance/DH_090399, accessed on 23 August 2012.

Campion, J. (1992) *Working with Vulnerable Young Children.* London: Cassell.

Cheshire Domestic Abuse Partnership (2005) Cheshire County Council publication.

Chung, Hyun Kyung (1996) 'Your Comfort versus My Death' in M. Mananzan et al. (eds) *Women Resisting Violence.* New York: Orbis.]

Cole, P., Martin, S. and Dennis, T. (2004) 'Emotion regulation as a scientific construction.' *Child Development 75,* 2, 317–333.

Collis, S. (2009) 'The analysis of stories of children and young people who have experienced domestic violence.' *International Journal of Children's Spirituality 14,* 4, 339–353.

Crompton, M. (1998) *Children, Spirituality and Social Work.* Aldershot: Ashgate.

Degenaar, J. (1991) *Book of Hope.* Cape Town: David Philip.

Denzin, N. (1989) *Interpretative Interactionism.* Newbury Park, CA: Sage.

Dorr, D. (1990) *Integral Spirituality.* New York: Orbis.

Ecclestone, K. and Hayes, D. (2009) 'Changing the subject: the educational implications of developing emotional wellbeing.' *Oxford Review of Education 35,* 3, 371–389.

Etherington, K. (2004) *Becoming a Reflexive Researcher.* London: Jessica Kingsley Publishers.

Fine, M. (1992) *Disruptive Voices: The Possibilities of Feminist Research.* Ann Arbor: University of Michigan Press.

Fine, M. (1997) *Readings on Race, Power and Society.* London: Routledge.

Fox M. (1990) *A Spirituality Named Compassion.* New York: Harper Collins.

Fox, M. (1991) *Creation Spirituality.* New York: Harper Collins.

Geen, R. (1990) *Human Aggression.* Milton Keynes: OU Press.

Goldstein, A. and Keller, H. (1987) *Aggressive Behaviour.* New York: Pergamon.

Goleman, D. (1995) *Emotional Intelligence.* London: Bloomsbury.

Goleman, D. (2005) *Emotional Intelligence.* New York: Bantam.

Gottlieb, R. (2003) *A Spirituality of Resistance.* London: Roman and Littlefield.

Graham, P. (2005) 'Cognitive behaviour therapies for children: passing fashion or here to stay?' *Child and Adolescent Mental Health 10*, 2, 57–62.

Greenhalgh, T. (1999) 'Why study narrative?' *British Medical Journal 318*, 48–50.

Grey, M. (1996) 'Epilogue.' In M. Manazan *et al.* (eds) *Women Resisting Violence.* New York: Orbis.

Grof, C. and Grof, S. (1990) *The Stormy Search for the Self.* New York: Tarcher/Penguin.

Grotberg, E. (1997) 'The International Resilience Project.' In M. John (ed.) *A Charge Against Society: A Child's Right to Protection.* London: Jessica Kingsley Publishers.

Hague, G., Malos E., Mullender, A., Kelly, L. and Imam, A. (2002) 'Children, coping strategies and domestic violence.' *Community Practitioner 75*, 5, 180–183.

Hester, M., Pearson, C. and Harwin, N. (2007) *Making an Impact: Children and Domestic Violence* (Second edition). London: Jessica Kingsley Publishers.

Holland, J., Blair, M. and Sheldon, S. (eds) (1995) *Debates and Issues in Feminist Research and Pedagogy.* Clevedon: Multilingual Matters in association with the Open University.

Israel, M. (1995) *Dark Victory: Through Depression to Hope.* London: Cassell.

Jessey, C. (1978) *Profiles in Hope.* London: Veritas.

Jessop, T. and Penny, A. (1999) 'A story behind a story: developing strategies for making sense of teacher narratives.' *International Journal of Social Research Methodology 12*, 3, 213–230.

Kane, J. (1997) 'Personal reflections on sources of illusions and hope.' *International Journal of Children's Spirituality 2*, 1, 5–8.

Kiesinger, C. (1998) 'From interview to story: writing Abbie's life.' *Qualitative Inquiry 4*, 1, 71–95.

King, U. (1996) 'Spirituality for Life.' In M. Manazan *et al.* (eds) *Women Resisting Violence.* New York: Orbis.

Krahe, B. (2001) *The Social Psychology of Aggression.* Hove: Psychology Press.

Larson, R. (2002) 'Continuity, stability and change in daily emotional experience across adolescence.' *Child Development 73*, 4, 1151–1165.

Leaman, O. (1995) *Death and Loss.* London: Cassell.

Lewis, M. and Granic, I. (eds) (2000) *Emotion, Development and Self Organisation.* Cambridge: Cambridge University Press.

Lieberman, A.F. (2004) 'Traumatic stress and quality of attachment reality and internalization in disorders of infant mental health.' *Infant Mental Health Journal 25*, 336–351.

Loades, M. and Mastroyannopoulou, K. (2010) 'Teachers' recognition of children's mental health problems.' *Children's and Adolescents' Mental Health 15*, 3, 150–156.

Mananzan, M., Oduyoye, M., Tamez, E., Clarkson, J., Grey, M. and Russell, L. (eds) (1996) *Women Resisting Violence.* New York: Orbis.

McCubbin, H., Thompson, E., Thompson, A. and Fromer, J. (1998) *Stress, Coping and Health.* California: Sage.

McKeating, H. (1970) *Living with Guilt.* London: SCM Press.

Mullender, A. (2005) *Tackling Domestic Violence: Providing Support for Children Who Have Witnessed Domestic Violence*. Development and Practice Report. London: Home Office.

Mullender, A., Hague, G., Imam, U., Kelly, L., Malos, E. and Regan, L. (2002) *Children's Perspectives on Domestic Violence*. London: Sage.

Murgatroyd, S. and Woolfe, R. (1982) *Coping with Crisis*. London: Harper and Row.

Newell, P. (2000) *Taking Children Seriously*. London: Calouste Gulbenkian Foundation.

Newman, T. (2004) *What Works in Building Resilience?* Essex: Barnardo's.

Oakley, K. and Jenkins, J. (1996) *Understanding Emotions*. Maldon: Blackwell.

Oduyoye, M. (1996) 'Spirituality of Resistance and Reconstruction.' In M. Mananzan *et al.* (eds) *Women Resisting Violence*. New York: Orbis.

Park, J. (1999) 'Emotional literacy: education for meaning.' *International Journal of Children's Spirituality 4*, 1, 19–28.

Peltomaki, D. (2008) 'An afflicted waiting.' *International Journal of Children's Spirituality 13*, 3, 223–233.

Philip, K. and Spratt, J. (2010) 'Choosing your friends: young people negotiating supportive relationships.' *Advances in School Mental Health Promotion 3*, 1, 42–51.

Pugmire, D. (1998) *Rediscovering Emotion*. Edinburgh: Edinburgh Press.

Rachman, S. (1998) *Anxiety*. Hove: Psychology Press.

Rentrew, J. (1997) *Aggression and its Causes*. Oxford: Oxford University Press.

Ribbens, J. and Edwards, R. (eds) (1998) *Feminist Dilemmas in Qualitative Research*. London: Sage.

Ridgway, R. (1973) *Aggression in Youth*. London: Priory Press.

Roberts, B. (2002) *Biographical Research*. Buckingham: Open University.

Robinson, S. (2008) *Spirituality, Ethics and Care*. London, Jessica Kingsley Publishers.

Rutter, M. (2004) (ed.) *Psycho-social Disturbances in Young People: Challenges for Prevention*. Cambridge: Cambridge University Press.

Seligman, M. (2007) *The Optimistic Child*. New York: Houghton Mifflin.

Sharp, S. and Cowie, H. (1998) *Counselling and Supporting Children in Distress*. London, Sage.

Spielberger, C., Borucki, A. and Sarason, I. (1991) *Stress and Emotion*. New York: Hemisphere.

Spratt, J., Philip, K., Shucksworth, J., Kiger, A. and Gair, D. (2010) 'We are the ones who talk about difficult subjects: nurses in schools working to support young people's mental health.' *Pastoral Care in Education, An International Journal of Pastoral, Social and Emotional Development 28*, 2, 131–144.

Stallard, P., Simpson, N., Anderson, S., Hibbert, S. and Osborn, C. (2007) 'The FRIENDS Emotional Health programme.' *Child and Adolescent Mental Health 12*, 1, 32–37.

Stolberg, T. (2008) 'Attending to the spiritual through the teaching of science: a study of pre-service primary teachers' attitudes.' *International Journal of Children's Spirituality 13*, 2, 171–180.

Strawson, P. (1974) *Freedom and Resentment*. London: Methuen.

Swinton, J. (2001) *Spirituality and Mental Health Care*. London: Jessica Kingsley Publishers.

Taylor, J., Gilligan, C. and Sullivan, A. (1995) *Between Voice and Silence*. Cambridge MA: Harvard University Press.

Uchtdorf, D. (2008) 'The infinite power of hope.' *The Church of Jesus Christ of Latter Day Saints, Ensign 38*, 11, 21–24.

Varma, V. (ed.) (1993) *How and Why Children Hate*. London: Jessica Kingsley Publishers.

Woods, G. and Woods, P. (2008) 'Democracy and spiritual awareness: interconnections and implications for educational leadership.' *International Journal of Children's Spirituality 13*, 2, 101–116.

Zappone, K. (1991) *The Hope for Wholeness*. Connecticut: Twenty-Third Publications.

Index